Oversize Shelf.

complete
thai
cooking

complete

thai

cooking

hamlyn

First published in Great Britain in 2006 by
Hamlyn, a division of Octopus Publishing Group Ltd
2–4 Heron Quays, London E14 4JP

ISBN-13: 978-0-600-61540-8
ISBN-10: 0-600-61540-5

A CIP catalogue record for this book is available from the British
Library

Printed and bound in China

10 9 8 7 6 5 4 3 2 1

Notes

Both metric and imperial measurements have been given in all recipes.
Use one set of measurements only, and not a mixture of both.

Standard level spoon measurements are used in all recipes.
1 tablespoon = one 15 ml spoon
1 teaspoon = one 5 ml spoon

Eggs should be large unless otherwise stated. The Department of Health advises that
eggs should not be consumed raw. This book contains dishes made with raw or lightly
cooked eggs. It is prudent for more vulnerable people such as pregnant and nursing
mothers, invalids, the elderly, babies and young children to avoid uncooked or lightly
cooked dishes made with eggs. Once prepared, these dishes should be kept refrigerated
and used promptly.

Milk should be full fat unless otherwise stated.

This book includes dishes made with nuts and nut derivatives. It is advisable for
customers with known allergic reactions to nuts and nut derivatives and those who may
be potentially vulnerable to these allergies such as pregnant and nursing mothers,
invalids, the elderly, babies and children to avoid dishes made with nuts and nut oils.
It is also prudent to check the labels of pre-prepared ingredients for the possible
inclusion of nut derivatives.

Pepper should be freshly ground black pepper unless otherwise stated.

Fresh herbs should be used, unless otherwise stated. If unavailable, use dried herbs as
an alternative, but halve the quantities stated.

Ovens should be preheated to the specified temperature – if using a fan-assisted oven,
follow the manufacturer's instructions for adjusting the time and the temperature.

Contents

Introduction

Thailand is a beautiful and fertile country, which produces some of the best food in the world, and there can be no doubt about the importance of good food to its people. From the moment you set foot in the country, your senses are assailed from all sides by the smells of delicious chicken and dried squid and of pungent spices and herbs, the sound of pestles thudding into mortars and cleavers chopping vegetables, and the sight of exotic fruits loaded on to stalls, while out of the corner of your eye you see a huge whoosh of flame reaching up around a wok and the cook laughing at your surprise.

The beauty of Thai food lies in its contrasts – hot, cool, sour, sweet, crunchy, soft, all with a wonderful citrus tang – and Thai cuisine and its ingredients have had a considerable impact on our own food in recent years. Greatly increased numbers of visitors to Thailand have been discovering for themselves the particular delights of Thailand's unique cuisine, and more and more Thais have been leaving home to set up restaurants all over the world, from Sydney to London, and Auckland to San Francisco.

Thailand is still overwhelmingly an agricultural country, and its major natural resource is its agricultural potential. Although the agricultural sector's contribution to the national GNP has declined considerably in the last 40 years because of the huge growth in manufacturing output, the food industry still employs two-thirds of the labour force and directly supports 60 per cent of the population. The good thing about countries like Thailand, where the agriculture is still largely unintensive, is the fabulous quality of what is produced.

Whether at home or in countries far away, Thais always base their cooking on fresh ingredients, and wherever they are they remain true to a typical Thai style; there is no compromising on authentic Thai recipes to suit the palates of the countries where their cooks happen to be. The importance of preparation and cooking of food in Thailand is one of the first things you notice on arrival there. Everyone appreciates good food, and there are restaurants and food stalls everywhere you look. Thailand's tropical monsoon climate is responsible for the abundance of fruit and vegetables, which includes varieties of everything we grow in the West and many, many more.

Thailand's geographical position at the heart of Southeast Asia means that its cooking has taken on and adapted to its own character and preferences the cuisines of countries around it, notably China and India, but also Malaysia and Indonesia. In addition, European traders seeking spices and other goods have influenced Thai cooking, and it was, in fact, the Portuguese who introduced the chilli to Thailand in the early 16th century. Today, the chilli is one of the most important ingredients in Thai cuisine. Cardamoms came from India by way of Burma, coriander and cumin arrived from the Middle East, tapioca from Central America and tomatoes from South America via Europe.

Thai cooking is not a pale imitation of other oriental styles, however. There are plenty of hot dishes, and cooks make great use of the Chinese wok, although Thai stir-fries tend to be lighter and more highly spiced than Chinese ones. Thai stir-fries are also free of the cornflour often used by the Chinese as a thickening agent.

The curries have a greater lightness of touch than those of India, allied to an aromatic sourness and a certain sweetness that is uniquely Thai. The basic ingredients of a Thai curry, which may be pork, beef, chicken or fish, or simple fresh vegetables, is cut into more delicate slivers than the chunks that are usual in Indian cooking, and the fiery taste comes from the pastes – red curry paste based on red chillies and green curry paste on green ones – that flavour them.

With the curry pastes are added fresh herbs, spices and other flavourings, which may include lemon grass, coriander (the leaves, stalks and root of fresh coriander are all used in Thai cooking, as well as the seeds), lime leaves, three types of basil, galangal, ginger, garlic and shallots.

Healthy eating

Over the last few years, we have all become increasingly aware of how food impacts on our health and the ways in which large-scale, industrialized food production affects our environment, often in terrible ways. More and more of us want to eat free-range eggs and organically grown vegetables. We are aware of the importance of eating locally produced, seasonally available foods that have not travelled halfway round the world to our shops. We are also increasingly aware of problems with pesticides, with nitrates in the water table and with our water supplies in general. We have begun to buy eco-friendly cleaning materials and washing powders, we recycle paper and bottles and we all want to live a life that is better for us and better for our planet. Cooking and eating Thai food is a delicious and unusual way of eating healthily.

The Thai diet is one of the healthiest in the world. There are plenty of fresh vegetables and fruit, good-quality rice and noodles and relatively small amounts of meat and fish. Dairy products are virtually unused by most Thai people, and cattle raising is on a small scale.

You are more likely to find pigs, chickens and ducks on farms and smallholdings than cattle, and this is reflected in the cooking.

The food includes several types of fruit and vegetables that are not regularly used in the West but that offer a surprising range of nutrients. Limes are a good source of vitamin C, and bean sprouts continue to grow and form nutrients after picking, unlike most other vegetables. A normal helping of mung bean sprouts provides about 75 per cent of the adult RDA of vitamin C and is also a good source of some of the B vitamins. Garlic helps to lower cholesterol and blood pressure. It also has antiviral and antibacterial properties. Papaya is not only a good source of vitamin C and betacarotene but also provides small amounts of calcium and iron as well. The juice contains papain, an enzyme similar to pepsin, which is produced by our digestive systems to break down proteins. Papain is very good for combating digestive disorders; indeed, the food industry uses papain as a natural meat tenderizer.

Thai cuisine

Thai eating is usually very relaxed, with six or eight dishes appearing in the centre of the table and everyone helping themselves to a small amount of each. There is always a big bowl of rice, which is so important to Thai people that their verb 'to eat' is literally 'eat rice'. In the northern, mountainous regions of Thailand, people eat a mountain rice, which does not require flooded paddy fields in which to grow. This rice is of poor quality, both in flavour and nutritionally. Sticky (glutinous) rice, which is short-grained, is the staple in the rest of northern and northeastern Thailand. The cuisine there is much drier. People use their fingers to eat with, making little balls of rice between their fingers and thumb and using these to scoop up the rest of the food. In central and southern

Thailand, sticky rice is mainly used in desserts. Although Thais like sweet things and make many dessert-type dishes, they actually eat them as snacks rather than at the end of the meal.

Fish is important in the Thai diet and always has been. The whole country is crossed by rivers and natural waterways, so freshwater fish and shellfish are readily available in places where fish from the sea is unobtainable. Much fish of all types is dried, salted or turned into shrimp paste or nam pla (fish sauce).

Forks and spoons are the usual implements with which to eat, unless the dish is noodles or a noodle soup, in which case chopsticks and a spoon are used. This use of chopsticks shows the influence of China, which goes back to the first century AD when the tribal T'ai people began to migrate from China down to Burma, Laos, Vietnam and Thailand. Here they joined other tribal people, whose main influences were Burmese and Cambodian, themselves both influenced by India. Over the next few centuries, first one and then another power waxed and waned, then in the 13th century the Kingdom of Sukhothai was formed. All the tribes absorbed ideas and languages from one another and gradually became a cohesive people in their own right. They were called Siamese, and the country became known as Siam. That name was officially changed to Thailand in 1949. All these influences were responsible for what we now know as Thai cuisine, and help to explain how it came to be as immensely varied and unique as it is.

There are not many vegetarian Thais, but their numbers are growing. One of Thailand's greatest sources of foreign exchange is the tourist trade and significant numbers of Western tourists are vegetarians, so it is now becoming quite easy to find wonderful and unusual

Dining Thai-style is an informal affair, with several different dishes served at about the same time, to which everyone helps themselves.

vegetarian food in Thailand. Specifically vegetarian food stalls exist in many markets, as does the occasional vegetarian restaurant. In addition, if you do not see what you want on a menu in a non-vegetarian restaurant, the chef will usually be happy to cook a vegetarian dish for you if you ask. You will find that the more you try to cook vegetarian Thai food, the quicker and easier it will be, and the more adventurous you will become.

Getting started

If you are thinking of experimenting with Thai food, your first step should be to visit an oriental food store or supermarket. Here you will be able to buy everything you need, in both food and equipment terms. Although most supermarkets and many corner shops carry some useful items, such as noodles, bamboo shoots and soy sauce, they cannot compete with the real thing. For example, Thai jasmine or fragrant rice can be bought in large sacks from oriental stores, and these will last a long time and will be considerably cheaper than buying the rice in individual boxes or bags of 500 g (1 lb).

Cooking Thai-style may seem a little alarming at first. So many small amounts of different things go into each dish, and somehow a number of different dishes have to be ready to eat at more or less the same time. The answer is to choose your menu carefully. Rice can be reheated easily in a steamer, and curries can also be cooked in advance and reheated. Soup can be cooked in a saucepan, leaving the wok free for deep-frying a fish or stir-frying, and salads can be prepared in advance and finished at the last moment.

As with any other form of cooking, the more often you do it the easier it becomes, until you find you can turn out inexpensive, nutritious meals at the drop of a hat.

Whether or not you become totally addicted to Thai food, you can be sure that when you prepare a Thai meal you will be eating healthily and enjoyably.

Equipment

Thai kitchens are extremely simple compared to the ones we are used to in the West, and it's probable that you will already have most of the equipment required to cook Thai food. The whole experience of Thai cooking is hands-on – there is lots of chopping and pounding and tearing, but most Thais do not have ovens, so they have not evolved the sort of long, slow casserole cooking or roasting that are features of Western cooking.

You will find a heavy kitchen cleaver useful for peeling (when you hold the blade held horizontally) or chopping vegetables, cutting through bones, opening pineapples and coconuts and finely chopping herbs (when you can use the whole blade), and don't forget a good-quality chopping board. Of course, you can also use kitchen knives, vegetable peelers and scissors equally well.

A bamboo-handled wire basket is useful for blanching vegetables, plunging noodles into stock or boiling water for a few moments to cook and for removing deep-fried food from the hot oil, although a slotted spoon does this last task perfectly well. A long-handled spatula, shaped rather like a shovel, is ideal for moving the ingredients around while your are stir-frying.

Wok

You will need a wok, preferably one with a wooden handle; some of the cheaper woks have metal handles, and you can burn yourself if you aren't careful. If you do not have a wok, you could use a large, nonstick frying pan. The advantage of a wok is the way the whole surface heats up, the hottest part being in the centre, allowing you to push ingredients to the side if you think they are almost done and to cook something else in the centre. Woks are also deep enough to hold plenty of liquid, so you can cook curries and deep-fry in them, as well as stir-fry.

Thai food is cooked fast. The ingredients are chopped into small pieces before you begin and cooked for a short time over a fairly high heat. They should all be slightly crunchy when they reach your mouth. Thai cooks work over a very high flame, very fast, and lift the wok off the flame when they want to reduce the temperature. When you first try cooking in a wok, a moderately high temperature will do; it will allow you to concentrate on the cooking and not waste precious moments adjusting the heat.

When you stir-fry, it is best to heat the wok, add a little oil, swirl it around and get it good and hot before you add your first ingredients. Think carefully about exactly what it is you are cooking and the order in which the ingredients should be added. Put more solid items, such as carrots and broccoli stalks, into the wok first, with the most delicate vegetables, such as small leaves or bean sprouts, which are cooked for just a few seconds, going in last. Don't be afraid to toss the food around in the wok; you need to keep moving it from the centre to the side and back again.

Steamer

You will also need a steamer, either a stainless steel one, which you will find very useful in your everyday cooking too, or a bamboo steamer of the kind you can find in oriental stores. You can rig up your own steamer easily enough by putting a metal colander over a saucepan of

boiling water. Line the colander with muslin if you want to steam rice, if you don't have an electric rice steamer. You can steam dumplings on a plate placed in the colander with a lid on top to trap the steam. Make sure that the water in the saucepan does not dry out.

The advantage of a bamboo steamer is that the steam does not condense on the lid and drip moisture on to the food below, which can spoil its appearance. If you are cooking something like a whole fish in a metal steamer, cover it with kitchen paper to protect it.

Food to be steamed is often wrapped in leaves, usually banana leaves, which not only imparts the flavour of the leaf to the food, but looks appealing when the food is brought to the table.

Pestle and mortar

If you want to produce curry pastes and sauces with an authentic texture, you will need a large pestle and mortar to blend chillies, garlic, onions and other spices together. However, you can use an electric food processor to good effect; indeed, many urban Thais use them these days. If you want to grind fresh, whole spices but don't have a pestle and mortar, you can use an electric coffee grinder, thoroughly cleaned both before and after use, or a spice grinder. If you are going to grind fresh spices on a regular basis, it would be worth buying either a pestle and mortar or a coffee grinder or spice grinder specifically for this purpose.

A large pestle and mortar is a must for pounding and grinding herbs and spices. Choose a heavy stoneware or marble variety.

Basic Recipes

At the heart of Thai cooking lie vitally important curry pastes and good stocks. The stocks and pastes described here are ideal for using in the recipes in this book.

Red Curry Paste

6 dried red chillies, deseeded, soaked, drained and roughly chopped

2 tablespoons chopped lemon grass or ¼ teaspoon grated lemon rind

1 teaspoon chopped fresh coriander root or stalk

1 tablespoon chopped shallots

1 tablespoon chopped garlic

1 teaspoon chopped fresh galangal or root ginger

2 teaspoons coriander seeds

1 teaspoon cumin seeds

6 white peppercorns

1 teaspoon salt

1 teaspoon shrimp paste

put all the ingredients in a food processor and process to a thick paste.

alternatively, put the chillies in a mortar and pound with a pestle, then add the lemon grass or lemon rind and pound it with the fresh coriander, and so on with all the remaining ingredients.

transfer the paste to an airtight container. Any that you do not use immediately may be stored in the refrigerator for up to 3 weeks.

Preparation time: *15 minutes*

Yellow Curry Paste

3 small fresh chillies (yellow or orange)

4 garlic cloves, halved

4 shallots, roughly chopped

3 teaspoons ground turmeric

I teaspoon salt

15 black peppercorns

I lemon grass stalk, chopped

2.5 cm (I inch) piece of fresh root ginger, peeled and chopped

put all the ingredients in a food processor and process to a thick paste.

alternatively, pound all the ingredients together in a mortar with a pestle.

transfer the paste to an airtight container. Any that you do not use immediately may be stored in the refrigerator for up to 3 weeks.

Preparation time: *15 minutes*

Green Curry Paste

15 small fresh green chillies

4 garlic cloves, halved

2 lemon grass stalks, finely chopped, or ¼ teaspoon grated lemon rind

2 kaffir lime leaves, torn

2 shallots, chopped

50 g (2 oz) fresh coriander leaves, stalks and roots

2.5 cm (I inch) piece of fresh root ginger, peeled and chopped

2 teaspoons coriander seeds

I teaspoon black peppercorns

I teaspoon finely grated lime rind

½ teaspoon salt

2 tablespoons groundnut oil

put all the ingredients in a food processor and process to a thick paste.

alternatively, put the chillies in a mortar and pound with a pestle, then add the garlic and pound it with the lemon grass or lemon rind, and so on with all the remaining ingredients, then mix in the oil with a spoon.

transfer the paste to an airtight container. Any that you do not use immediately may be stored in the refrigerator for up to 3 weeks.

Preparation time: *15 minutes*

Chicken Stock

1.75 kg (3½ lb) whole chicken

500 g (1 lb) chicken giblets

1 onion, halved

1 carrot, roughly chopped

2 celery sticks, including leaves, roughly chopped

1.8 litres (3 pints) cold water

2 garlic cloves

1 lemon grass stalk, roughly chopped, or ¼ teaspoon grated lemon rind

1 kaffir lime leaf

10 black peppercorns

3 large fresh red chillies

put the chicken in a large, heavy-based saucepan or casserole with the giblets, onion, carrot and celery and pour over the measurement water until the ingredients are just covered. Put the pan over a very low heat and bring it to the boil as slowly as possible. Reduce the heat and simmer for about 50 minutes. When the liquid begins to simmer, remove the scum that rises to the surface until only white foam rises.

add all the remaining ingredients, cover and simmer gently for 2 hours. Use a heat diffuser if you need to.

remove the chicken and set aside for another use. Strain the stock without pressing the juices from the vegetables – this helps to keep it clear. Use as much as you need immediately, quickly cooling and freezing the remainder for future use.

Makes about 1.5 litres (2½ pints)
Preparation time: *5 minutes*
Cooking time: *about 3 hours*

Beef Stock

1.8 litres (3 pints) cold water

400 g (13 oz) beef or veal bones with some meat on, roughly chopped

1 carrot, roughly chopped

1 celery stick, roughly chopped

1 onion, quartered

2.5 cm (1 inch) piece of fresh root ginger, peeled and sliced

2 coriander plants, including roots

5 black peppercorns, crushed

put all the ingredients in a large saucepan and bring to the boil. Reduce the heat and simmer for 1½ hours. From time to time skim off any fat that rises to the surface.

strain the stock into a clean bowl, discard the solids and other unwanted parts and leave to cool.

cover the stock and leave in the refrigerator for 4–5 hours or overnight. Remove any fat that has solidified on the surface.

Makes about 900 ml (1½ pints)
Preparation time: *10 minutes, plus cooling and chilling*
Cooking time: *about 1½ hours*

Vegetable Stock

2 large onions, quartered

4 large fresh red chillies

250 g (8 oz) carrots, halved

¼ small white cabbage, halved

1 small head of celery, including leaves, chopped

50 g (2 oz) fresh coriander leaves, stalks and roots

25 g (1 oz) basil leaves and stalks

½ head of Chinese leaves, chopped

½ mooli or 6 radishes, peeled

25 black peppercorns

½ teaspoon salt

1 teaspoon palm sugar or light muscovado sugar

2 litres (3½ pints) water

put all the ingredients in a heavy-based saucepan or casserole. Bring to the boil, then reduce the heat, cover and simmer for 1 hour.

remove the lid and boil hard for 10 minutes. Leave the stock to cool, then strain. Use as much as you need immediately, quickly cooling and freezing the remainder for future use.

Makes about 1.8 litres (3 pints)
Preparation time: *5–10 minutes, plus cooling*
Cooking time: *about 1¼ hours*

Fish Stock

500 g (1 lb) raw white fish heads and bones, and prawn heads and shells, if available

2.5 litres (4 pints) cold water

3 shallots

1 celery stick, including leaves, roughly chopped

1 kaffir lime leaf

½ lemon grass stalk or ¼ teaspoon grated lemon rind

2 garlic cloves

25 g (1 oz) fresh coriander stalks and roots

put the fish trimmings and measurement water into a large, heavy-based saucepan and bring to the boil. Skim off any scum that rises to the surface.

add the shallots, celery, lime leaf, lemon grass or lemon rind, garlic and coriander, cover and simmer for 50 minutes.

strain the stock and use as much as you need immediately, quickly cooling and freezing the remainder for future use.

Makes about 2 litres (3½ pints)
Preparation time: *5 minutes*
Cooking time: *about 1 hour*

Cook's Terms

As Thai cuisine has gained in popularity outside Thailand, first oriental food stores, then supermarkets and now many small, local shops sell an increasing range of Thai ingredients. Most of the ingredients used in this book are readily available, but alternatives are included for the more unusual items wherever possible. It is worth paying a little extra for your ingredients to make sure that they taste as good as they should.

Bamboo shoots

The young, ivory-coloured, conical-shaped shoots of edible bamboo plants are tender and crunchy, and add texture and sweetness to many dishes. Bamboo shoots are available canned, fresh and sometimes vacuum-packed.

Banana leaves

These can be found in oriental food stores and are used to contain food during steaming and grilling. You can use foil or small bowls, depending on your needs, but banana leaves are more authentic and look spectacular. They also impart a faint flavour.

Basil

Holy basil is used as often as sweet (European) basil in Thai cookery. With smaller, darker leaves and purple stalks, it is less sweet than European basil, which may be used instead.

Bean sauce

Black, yellow and red bean sauces made from preserved soya beans are available in jars. Black beans are available in cans and bags and should be rinsed and chopped before use. Unused beans and their liquid can be stored indefinitely if kept in a sealed container in the refrigerator. Bean sauce and beans can be bought from most supermarkets and oriental food stores.

Bitter melon

This has a fairly pale green, lumpy skin and is found in oriental food stores. It has a very bitter taste, but you can use marrow, courgette or cucumber if you prefer.

Chillies

There are so many different kinds of chilli that it would be difficult to list them all. As a rule, the smaller the chilli the fiercer the heat, and red chillies are slightly less fierce because they become sweeter as they ripen. Most of the heat of chillies is contained in and around the seeds and the inner membrane. Thai cooks often include the seeds, but you may prefer to remove them for a milder flavour. Fresh orange and yellow chillies are often used in Thai cooking as much for their pretty colours as for their flavour. You can occasionally buy them from specialist oriental stores and markets, but otherwise use whatever colour you can get. See also page 148.

Coconut milk and cream

These are widely available in cans, packets and blocks (which require added water). You can make coconut milk yourself from desiccated coconut: place 175 g (6 oz) coconut in a food processor or blender with 300 ml (½ pint) hand-hot water; blend for 30 seconds and strain the liquid through muslin, squeezing it as dry as you can. This will produce thick coconut milk. If you repeat the process, then mix the two extractions, you will get a medium-thick coconut milk, suitable for most dishes. If you put this milk in the refrigerator, the 'cream' will rise to the surface and can be taken off. Coconut milk lasts only 1–2 days, even in the refrigerator. If you are using coconut cream, stir it constantly while cooking because it curdles easily.

Coriander

An essential ingredient in Thai cooking. All of the herb is used – the leaves, stalks and roots. Roots can be stored in an airtight container in the refrigerator or freezer.

Curry paste

Ready-made pastes are available in jars and packets, or make your own (see pages 12–13). They freeze perfectly.

Fragrant rice

The main rice of Thailand is jasmine rice or Thai fragrant rice. If Thai fragrant rice is not available, any good-quality long-grain rice, especially basmati, would suit the recipes in this book very well.

Galangal

This is a root similar to ginger, but the skin is thinner and slightly pink, and the taste is milder. It is available in large supermarkets and oriental food stores. It is peeled before use, then either sliced or chopped according to the recipe. Dried slices are also available, and 1 dried slice is the equivalent of 1 cm (½ inch) of the fresh root.

Garlic

White garlic is a main ingredient in Thai cooking and is used in many dishes. The size of the clove doesn't really affect the flavour, although the largest cloves are milder.

Ginger

Fresh root ginger is readily available. Use it in the same way as galangal, as described below left.

Krachai

Also called lesser ginger, this root is smaller and fiercer than ginger and galangal, but it comes from the same family and should be treated in the same way. It is usually available dried in packets.

Lemon grass

Widely available from supermarkets in bundles of 4–6 stalks, the straw-like tops should be trimmed as well as the ends, and the stalks thinly sliced. If you can't get fresh lemon grass, dried and ground lemon grass is available, or you can use lemon rind or juice instead.

Limes and lime leaves

The type of lime grown in Thailand is called kaffir. Kaffir lime leaves can be bought fresh or dried in oriental food stores and large supermarkets, but if you cannot find them, use lime rind or juice.

Lemon grass is one of the most popular herbs of Southeast Asia and is a vital flavour in Thai curry pastes.

Mushrooms

Several types of mushroom are used in Thai dishes. Dried black fungus (cloud ear, mouse ear or wood fungus) can be found in packets in oriental food stores. Soak them in warm water for 15–20 minutes and drain them before use. Oyster mushrooms are available fresh from most supermarkets. Shiitake mushrooms can be found dried in oriental food stores, health food stores and some supermarkets, which also sell them fresh occasionally. If dried, they should be soaked in warm water for 15–20 minutes before use, then the hard stalk cut away and added to the stockpot. Shiitake are expensive, but you only need to use a few at a time. Straw mushrooms can be found in cans from supermarkets. Button, chestnut and field mushrooms can be used if none of the other types are available.

Nam pla (fish sauce) is a clear brown liquid, famous for its pungent aroma and strong, salty flavour.

Nam pla (fish sauce)

This essential ingredient in Thai cooking is widely available in supermarkets. It is a clear brown liquid, sold in bottles, made from pulverized, fermented, salted fish (usually anchovies). It has a strong flavour and pungent aroma. Although it is a contradiction in terms, there is a vegetarian 'fish' sauce, which is sometimes available in large oriental food stores or vegetarian stores. If you cannot find it, use light soy sauce or salt.

Noodles

Many kinds of noodle are used in Thai cooking, but the most commonly available are egg noodles, rice vermicelli, rice sticks and glass noodles. Egg noodles can be bought fresh from oriental stores, but the dried ones, which are widely available at supermarkets, are just as good. Rice vermicelli are very thin, white and translucent. Rice sticks are the same as vermicelli, only wider and flatter. They come in varying widths, and it is a matter of personal preference which ones you choose. Glass noodles, also known as cellophane noodles, bean thread noodles and bean vermicelli, are similar to rice vermicelli but are made from mung beans.

Oriental greens

Thai cooks use many different green vegetables, including pak choi, choi sum, Chinese cabbage and Chinese leaves. Chinese broccoli is available fresh at oriental stores. It is similar to European sprouting broccoli except that it is longer and thinner, with more stalk and less floret. The stalk is the most interesting part, and it is sliced and cooked in many ways.

Palm sugar

This soft, raw light brown sugar is widely used in Southeast Asia. In Thailand it is often sold wet, giving it a thick, honey-like consistency, but it is exported in hard blocks, which can be broken into pieces and dissolved. It tastes delicious and is attractive in desserts. If you can't get it, use a light muscovado or Indian jaggery sugar.

Papaya

Also called pawpaw, this tropical fruit is available from supermarkets. When unripe, the pale green, slightly bitter flesh is used in salads. The orange flesh of ripe papaya tastes best with a little lime juice.

Shrimp paste

Available 'fresh' or dried in plastic tubs or wrapped blocks, this strongly smelling ingredient is made of salted, decomposed shrimp. Dried blocks are stronger than the 'fresh' variety. Shrimp paste is available from oriental food stores.

Soy sauce

Soy sauce is made from fermented soya beans. Light soy sauce is used in the recipes in this book, unless otherwise indicated. Dark soy sauce is not only darker in colour but is also thicker and slightly sweeter than light soy sauce.

Spring roll wrappers

White and flimsy, these are made from flour and water and are usually square. Buy them ready-made, fresh or frozen in plastic bags, from oriental supermarkets. They are fragile, so handle them gently. If you can't find the shape of wrapper you need for a recipe, buy whatever you can and cut to the required shape. If you cannot find them, use sheets of filo pastry and cut them to size.

Sticky rice

A type of short-grain rice, sometimes called glutinous rice, that is used in many Thai desserts. It is opaque and must be steamed. For best results, always soak for several hours or even overnight before cooking.

Tamarind

Dried tamarind pulp can be found in oriental and Indian food stores. To make tamarind water, simmer the pulp for 2–3 minutes, leave to cool, then squeeze out the juice and discard the pulp and seeds. Tamarind concentrate can be bought in tubs; dissolve a spoonful in hot water. You can substitute lemon juice.

Tofu

There are several kinds of tofu (beancurd), which is made from soya beans. Fresh white tofu is sold in blocks in its own liquid. It is very delicate and will break up if stirred too much. Blocks of ready-fried tofu are much more solid. They are ideal for stir-frying. You can buy fairly solid white tofu cakes packed in water in plastic containers; these can be used for stir-frying if you can't get the ready-fried kind. All of these products are available from health food stores, supermarkets and oriental food stores.

Turmeric

This spice is a golden-yellow colourant with a mild flavour. It can sometimes be found fresh in oriental food stores but is most often used in its dried, ground form.

Vinegar

It is worth looking for white rice vinegar or distilled white vinegar in large supermarkets or oriental stores. Cider vinegar is an acceptable alternative, but do not use malt vinegar, which does not suit oriental food.

Wonton wrappers

Made from flour and eggs, these are deep yellow or golden-brown in colour. They are sold ready-made, fresh or frozen, in plastic bags from oriental food stores. If a recipe uses differently shaped wrappers, cut them to shape with scissors. Alternatively, use sheets of filo pastry cut to the required shape.

Snacks and Starters

Crispy Wrapped Prawns

Spring roll wrappers are widely available in oriental stores. They are delicate, so handle them gently and carefully cut them to size if you can only find larger ones.

75 g (3 oz) minced pork

4 raw prawns, peeled and finely chopped, plus 12 raw whole prawns, unpeeled

½ teaspoon palm sugar or light muscovado sugar

¼ onion, finely chopped

1 garlic clove, finely chopped

2 teaspoons soy sauce

12 spring roll wrappers, each about 12 cm (5 inches) square

egg white, beaten, for sealing

about 750 ml (1¼ pints) oil, for deep-frying

basil or fresh coriander sprigs, to garnish

To serve
lime wedges
Hot Sweet Sauce (see page 246)

mix together the pork, chopped prawns, sugar, onion, garlic and soy sauce in a bowl.

peel the 12 whole prawns, leaving the shell on the tails intact, and carefully cut open, making sure that you do not cut right through them.

put 1–2 teaspoons of the pork and prawn mixture on to each opened prawn. Spread out a spring roll wrapper on a work surface and pull one corner about three-quarters of the way towards the opposite corner. Place a prawn on the double thickness of the wrapper, leaving the tail free, and roll it up, tucking the ends in and sealing with a little egg white. Repeat until all prawns are wrapped.

heat the oil in a wok or deep frying pan to 180–190°C (350–375°F), or until a cube of bread browns in 30 seconds. Deep-fry the prawn rolls, in 2 batches if necessary, for about 5 minutes, or until golden-brown. Remove with a slotted spoon and drain on kitchen paper. Garnish with basil or coriander sprigs and serve with lime wedges and the hot sweet sauce.

Serves 4
Preparation time: *10–15 minutes*
Cooking time: *5–10 minutes*

Chicken Satay

Satay (or satei) sauce arrived in Thailand from Indonesia and often accompanies pork and beef as well as chicken. Use peanuts in the sauce for an authentic flavour.

500 g (1 lb) boneless, skinless chicken breast, cut into 2.5–5 cm (1–2 inch) pieces

Marinade

1 tablespoon ground cinnamon

1 tablespoon ground cumin

1 teaspoon pepper

150 ml (¼ pint) groundnut oil

100 ml (3½ fl oz) soy sauce

2 tablespoons palm sugar or light muscovado sugar

Satay sauce

1 heaped teaspoon Red Curry Paste (see page 12)

1 tablespoon groundnut oil

250 ml (8 fl oz) coconut milk

50 g (2 oz) palm sugar or light muscovado sugar

25 ml (1 fl oz) nam pla (fish sauce)

juice of 1 lime

65 g (2½ oz) Crushed Roasted Nuts – use peanuts (see page 248)

1 teaspoon crushed dried chillies

To garnish

roughly chopped onion

cucumber chunks

make the marinade. Mix all the marinade ingredients together in a bowl. Add the chicken pieces and turn in the marinade to coat thoroughly. Cover and leave to marinate in the refrigerator for at least 4 hours, preferably overnight, stirring occasionally.

make the satay sauce. Put the curry paste in a saucepan with the oil and stir over a low heat for 1 minute. Add the remaining sauce ingredients and cook over a moderate heat until thickened and blended. Remove from the heat, turn the sauce into a serving bowl and leave to cool.

carefully thread the chicken pieces on to bamboo skewers, presoaked in cold water for 1 hour, leaving some space at either end. Cook under a preheated hot grill, in batches, for about 2 minutes, turning once. You cannot see if the chicken is cooked through, so test one piece, grilling it for a little longer if necessary. Keep the cooked chicken warm while you cook the remaining skewers.

garnish the skewers with chopped onion and cucumber chunks and serve with the satay sauce.

Serves 4
Preparation time: *20 minutes, plus marinating*
Cooking time: *about 15 minutes*

Prawn and Corn Fritters

Many types of dipping sauce accompany Thai meals. Offer them in separate small bowls so that diners can experiment with the different flavours.

20 g (¾ oz) self-raising flour

65 g (2½ oz) raw peeled prawns, finely chopped

1 teaspoon Red Curry Paste (see page 12)

50 g (2 oz) canned, drained sweetcorn kernels

1 egg white

1 kaffir lime leaf, shredded

oil, for deep-frying

fresh coriander sprigs, to garnish (optional)

Hot Sweet Sauce (see page 246), to serve

Soy and vinegar dipping sauce

3 tablespoons distilled white vinegar or Chinese rice vinegar

3 tablespoons dark soy sauce

1½ teaspoons caster sugar

2 small fresh chillies, finely sliced

make the dipping sauce. Mix all the sauce ingredients together in a bowl and stir until the sugar dissolves. Set aside.

mix together the flour, prawns, curry paste, sweetcorn kernels, egg white and lime leaf in a separate bowl.

heat the oil in a wok or deep frying pan to 180–190°C (350–375°F), or until a cube of bread browns in 30 seconds. Drop 1 heaped tablespoon of the fritter mixture at a time into the hot oil, in 2 batches if necessary, and deep-fry for about 5 minutes, or until golden-brown. Remove with a slotted spoon and drain on kitchen paper. Transfer to a serving dish.

garnish with coriander sprigs, if liked, and serve with the dipping sauce and the hot sweet sauce.

Serves 4
Preparation time: *10 minutes*
Cooking time: *5–10 minutes*

Steamed Wonton

Wonton wrappers are widely available in oriental food stores, but if you cannot find them, you could use spring roll wrappers or filo pastry instead. Cut the sheets to size and cover them with a damp tea towel while you work.

16 wonton wrappers

oil, for drizzling

Filling

6 raw prawns, peeled

125 g (4 oz) minced pork

40 g (1½ oz) onion, finely chopped

2 garlic cloves, finely chopped

5 canned, drained water chestnuts, finely chopped

1 teaspoon palm sugar or light muscovado sugar

1 tablespoon soy sauce

1 egg

To serve

Soy and Vinegar Dipping Sauce (see page 26)

Hot Sweet Sauce (see page 246)

make the filling. Mix all the filling ingredients together in a bowl to form a thick paste.

put 1 heaped teaspoonful of the filling in the centre of a wonton wrapper, placed over your thumb and index finger. As you push the filled wrapper down through the circle that your fingers form, tighten the top, shaping it but leaving the top open. Repeat with the remaining wrappers.

put the filled wontons on a plate and place the plate in a steamer. Drizzle a little oil on top of the wontons, cover and steam for 30 minutes.

serve the wontons either hot or warm with the dipping sauce and the hot sweet sauce.

Makes 16
Preparation time: *15 minutes*
Cooking time: *30 minutes*

Toasted Chilli Cashew Nuts

250 g (8 oz) unroasted, unsalted cashew nuts

1 tablespoon groundnut oil

1 garlic clove, finely chopped

¼ teaspoon crushed dried chillies

1 spring onion, finely chopped

2 small fresh chillies (different colours), finely chopped

salt

dry-fry the cashew nuts in a wok or frying pan, using no oil, stirring constantly until golden brown. Remove from the heat and leave to cool.

heat the oil in a wok or large frying pan over a moderate heat and stir-fry the garlic for 1 minute, or until golden. Remove with a slotted spoon and set aside.

add the nuts to the oil and sprinkle over the crushed dried chillies. Stir-fry for 1 minute, then add the spring onion, chopped fresh chillies, garlic and salt to taste and stir-fry briefly. Serve warm.

Serves 4
Preparation time: 5 minutes
Cooking time: 5 minutes

clipboard: Chillies are an essential element in Thai cooking. Dried chillies are hotter than fresh ones, and just 1 or 2 small dried red chillies or a small quantity of crushed dried chillies or chilli flakes will add a significant amount of heat.

Raw Vegetables with Yellow Bean Sauce

about 500 g (1 lb) mixed raw vegetables of your choice, such as carrots, red and orange peppers and cucumber

to garnish

1 fresh red chilli, sliced into rings

flowering chives (optional)

Yellow bean sauce

125 g (4 oz) yellow bean sauce

½ onion, chopped

1 tablespoon tamarind water (see right)

200 ml (7 fl oz) coconut milk

200 ml (7 fl oz) water

2 eggs

3 tablespoons palm sugar or light muscovado sugar

1 tablespoon soy sauce

cut all the vegetables into bite-sized pieces.

make the sauce. Put the yellow bean sauce and onion in a food processor and process until blended. Turn into a saucepan. Add the remaining sauce ingredients and bring slowly to the boil over a low heat, stirring. Remove from the heat and pour the sauce into a serving bowl.

garnish the sauce with the sliced red chilli and serve warm with the prepared vegetables, garnished with flowering chives, if liked.

Serves 4
Preparation time: *15 minutes*
Cooking time: *5–6 minutes*

clipboard: Tamarind has a distinctive, rather sour flavour. It is obtained from the seed pods of a tree that originated in Africa but that was widely planted in India before being cultivated commercially. The pulp from the pods is used in Thai cooking. Simmer dried pulp for 2–3 minutes, cool, then squeeze out the juice (discarding the pulp and seeds). Alternatively, dissolve a spoonful of concentrate in hot water.

Stuffed Green Peppers

8 large green peppers

about 750 ml (1¼ pints) groundnut oil, for deep-frying

chives, to garnish

Filling

3 baby corn cobs, roughly chopped

3 garlic cloves, halved

4 tablespoons groundnut oil

½ large onion, finely chopped

1 tomato, diced

2 fresh shiitake mushrooms, finely sliced

50 g (2 oz) green beans, finely sliced

½ teaspoon palm sugar or light muscovado sugar

1 tablespoon soy sauce

¼ teaspoon salt

1 teaspoon pepper

2 eggs

Batter

3 tablespoons cornflour

50 ml (2 fl oz) water

½ teaspoon salt

¼ teaspoon pepper

cut the tops off the peppers, remove the cores and seeds and set the hollow peppers aside.

make the filling. Put the baby corn and garlic in a food processor and process until blended.

heat 3 tablespoons of the oil in a wok or large frying pan over a moderately high heat and stir-fry the onion for 30 seconds. Add the tomato and mushrooms and stir-fry for 1 minute. Add the green beans and stir-fry for 30 seconds then add the corn and garlic mixture, the sugar, soy sauce, salt and pepper. At this point you may need to add the remaining oil.

break the eggs into the mixture and stir well. Cook for 2 minutes, then remove the pan from the heat and turn the mixture on to a plate. Stuff the peppers with the filling, making sure that they are as full as possible.

make the batter. Beat all the batter ingredients together in a bowl. Heat the oil in a wok or deep frying pan to 180–190°C (350–375°F), or until a cube of bread browns in 30 seconds. Coat half the peppers in the batter, drop them into the hot oil and deep-fry, moving them around gently, for 6–7 minutes until golden brown on all sides. Remove with a slotted spoon and drain on kitchen paper. Repeat with the remaining peppers and batter.

arrange the cooked peppers on a serving plate, garnish with chives and serve immediately.

Makes 8
Preparation time: *25 minutes*
Cooking time: *12–14 minutes*

Thai Egg Strips

Omelettes are popular snacks in Thailand, widely available in markets and from roadside vendors. This is a quick and easy dish, but looks impressive.

3 eggs, beaten

I shallot, finely sliced

green shoots of I spring onion, sliced

1–2 small fresh red chillies, finely chopped

I tablespoon chopped fresh coriander leaves

I tablespoon groundnut oil

salt and pepper

very fine strips of spring onion, to garnish (optional)

mix together all the ingredients, except the oil, in a bowl.

heat the oil in a wok or large frying pan over a moderately high heat, pour in the egg mixture and swirl it around the pan to form a large, thin omelette. Cook for 1–2 minutes until firm.

slide the omelette out on to a plate and roll it up as though it were a pancake. Leave to cool.

when the omelette is cool, cut the roll crossways into 5 mm (¼ inch) or 1 cm (½ inch) sections, depending on how wide you want your strips to be. Serve them, still rolled up or straightened out, in a heap, garnished with very fine strips of spring onion, if liked.

Serves 4
Preparation time: *5 minutes*
Cooking time: *2–3 minutes*

Son-in-law Eggs

Palm sugar, derived from the coconut palm and available in blocks or cans, is widely used in Southeast Asian cooking. Use light muscovado sugar if you cannot find palm sugar.

4 hard-boiled eggs

about 750 ml (1¼ pints) groundnut oil, for deep-frying

5 shallots, finely sliced

3 large garlic cloves, finely sliced

75 ml (3 fl oz) tamarind water (see page 32)

50 ml (2 fl oz) vegetarian nam pla (fish sauce) or 1 teaspoon salt

65 g (2½ oz) palm sugar or light muscovado sugar

100 ml (3½ fl oz) water

To garnish

2 large fresh red chillies, deseeded and diagonally sliced

fresh coriander leaves

shell the eggs and cut them in half lengthways.

heat the oil in a wok or large frying pan over a moderate heat and stir-fry the shallots and garlic until golden. Remove with a slotted spoon, drain on kitchen paper and set aside.

slide the eggs, yolk side down, into the hot oil. Cook until golden all over. Remove with a slotted spoon, drain on kitchen paper and set aside.

put the tamarind water, nam pla or salt and sugar in a saucepan. Stir until the sugar dissolves, then add the measurement water. Cook, stirring constantly, for 5 minutes, or until the sauce becomes syrupy. Reduce the heat.

arrange the eggs, yolk side up, on a plate and sprinkle over the shallots and garlic. Bring the sauce to a fast boil and continue boiling until it is reduced and thickened. Remove from the heat and ladle over the eggs.

serve hot, garnished with the sliced red chillies and coriander leaves.

Serves 4
Preparation time: *20 minutes*
Cooking time: *15 minutes*

Fried Golden Bags

If necessary, you can make the little pouches up to about three hours in advance, keeping them covered in the refrigerator. You can also freeze the filled, uncooked pouches.

20 wonton wrappers (suitable for frying), each about 12 cm (5 inches) square

20 flowering chives, about 10 cm (4 inches) long, plus extra to garnish

oil, for deep-frying

Plum Sauce (see page 46) or Chilli Sauce (see page 138), to serve

Filling

75 g (3 oz) canned, drained water chestnuts, chopped

250 g (8 oz) crab meat

50 g (2 oz) raw prawns, peeled and finely chopped

2 teaspoons Garlic Mixture (see page 250)

2 spring onions, chopped

1 fresh green chilli, deseeded and chopped

1 tablespoon dark soy sauce

1 tablespoon nam pla (fish sauce)

make the filling. Mix all the filling ingredients together in a large bowl to form a thick paste.

spread out the wonton wrappers on a work surface and divide the crab meat filling equally between them, putting a spoonful in the centre of each wrapper. Pull the 4 corners up into the centre to make little bags.

use the chives to secure the little bags around the centre where the corners of the wrappers are gathered together. Take care that the chives do not break as you tie them.

heat the oil in a wok or deep frying pan to 180–190°C (350–375°F), or until a cube of bread browns in 30 seconds. Deep-fry the little bags, a few at a time, for 2–3 minutes until crisp and golden brown. Remove with a slotted spoon and drain on kitchen paper.

serve very hot with plum sauce or chilli sauce, garnished with a few extra flowering chives.

Serves 4–5
Preparation time: *25 minutes*
Cooking time: *8–12 minutes*

Thai Prawn Toasts

Mooli comes from the same vegetable family as the radish, which can be used instead, but it is much larger and has a slightly less peppery taste.

75 g (3 oz) raw prawns, peeled and finely chopped

125 g (4 oz) minced pork

1 tablespoon fresh coriander leaves, finely chopped, plus extra to garnish

1 tablespoon finely chopped spring onion

1 teaspoon Garlic Mixture (see page 250)

1 tablespoon nam pla (fish sauce)

1 egg, beaten

5 slices white bread

5 tablespoons sesame seeds

oil, for deep-frying

Plum sauce

5 tablespoons distilled white vinegar or Chinese rice vinegar

4 tablespoons plum jam

1 small fresh red chilli, finely sliced

To serve

¼ green pepper, thinly sliced

ribbons of raw mooli

make the plum sauce. Put the vinegar and jam in a small saucepan and heat gently, mixing thoroughly. Remove the pan from the heat, turn the sauce into a small serving bowl and leave to cool. Add the chilli before serving.

put the prawns and pork into a bowl with the coriander, spring onion, garlic mixture and nam pla. Add the egg and mix well.

cut each slice of bread into 4 roughly equal pieces and spread each one with some of the prawn and pork mixture, using a knife to press the mixture firmly on to the bread. Sprinkle the sesame seeds on top.

heat about 2.5 cm (1 inch) of oil in a wok or deep frying pan to 180–190°C (350–375°F), or until a cube of bread browns in 30 seconds. Deep-fry the pieces of bread, a few at a time, topping side down, for 6–8 minutes, then turn them over and cook the other side until golden brown. Remove with a slotted spoon and drain on kitchen paper.

garnish with chopped coriander and serve hot with the plum sauce, thin slices of green pepper and ribbons of mooli.

Serves 4
Preparation time: *15 minutes*
Cooking time: *8–10 minutes*

Deep-fried Corn Cakes

Soy sauce, made from fermented soy beans, is an essential ingredient in almost all Asian cuisines, and it is available in all supermarkets and large food stores.

500 g (1 lb) corn cobs

500 g (1 lb) minced pork (not too lean)

1 tablespoon Garlic Mixture (see page 250)

2 eggs, beaten

2 tablespoons plain flour

1 tablespoon cornflour

1 teaspoon salt

2 tablespoons soy sauce

½ vegetable stock cube, crumbled (optional)

oil, for deep-frying

2 tablespoons fresh coriander leaves, chopped, to garnish

To serve

1 large cucumber, very thinly sliced

12 fresh red chillies, deseeded and cut into very fine strips

working over a bowl, slice the kernels off the corn cobs with a sharp knife. Add the pork and garlic mixture and mix well, then stir in half the beaten egg.

add the flour, cornflour, salt and soy sauce, stirring well to make a mixture that is firm enough to be shaped. Add more beaten egg if necessary. Break off a small piece of the mixture and test-fry it in a little oil. If it tastes bland, mix in the crumbled stock cube.

form the mixture into flat, round cakes, each about 3.5 cm (1½ inches) across. Heat the oil in a wok or deep frying pan to 180–190°C (350–375°F), or until a cube of bread browns in 30 seconds Deep-fry the cakes, a few at a time, until cooked and golden brown. Remove with a slotted spoon and drain on kitchen paper. Leave to cool.

arrange the corn cakes on a serving plate and garnish with chopped coriander. Serve with cucumber slices and very fine strips of red chilli.

Serves 4
Preparation time: *15 minutes*
Cooking time: *20 minutes*

Griddled Prawn Cakes

Do not use instant mashed potato for this dish or the cakes will disintegrate when you fry them.

500 g (1 lb) cooked peeled prawns

1 garlic clove, crushed

2.5 cm (1 inch) piece of fresh root ginger, peeled and diced

2 fresh red chillies, chopped

1 bunch of fresh coriander, chopped

2 teaspoons nam pla (fish sauce)

1 egg yolk

250 g (8 oz) mashed potatoes

plain flour, for dusting (optional)

soy sauce or Chilli Sauce (see page 138), to serve

put the prawns in a food processor with the garlic, ginger, chillies, coriander, nam pla and egg yolk and process until smooth.

transfer the prawn mixture to a bowl, add the mashed potatoes and use a fork to mix together thoroughly. Form the mixture into 12 cakes, or 24 smaller ones if you prefer, dusting your hands in flour if the mixture is sticky.

heat a griddle pan over a moderately high heat. Cook the prawn cakes, in 2 batches, on the griddle for 5 minutes on each side. Keep the cooked cakes warm while you cook the remaining prawn cakes.

serve hot with some soy or chilli sauce.

Serves 4
Preparation time: *10 minutes*
Cooking time: *20 minutes*

Grilled Prawns and Scallops with Pineapple

300 g (10 oz) raw prawns, peeled and deveined

300 g (10 oz) raw scallops, shelled and cleaned

I fresh pineapple, cut into 25 x 2.5 cm (I inch) cubes

marinade

2 garlic cloves, finely chopped

I tablespoon finely chopped fresh coriander leaves

I long fresh red chilli, deseeded and finely chopped

I tablespoon sesame oil

I½ tablespoons light soy sauce

½ teaspoon ground white pepper

make the marinade. Mix all the marinade ingredients together in a bowl. Add the prawns and scallops and turn in the marinade to coat thoroughly. Cover and leave to marinate in the refrigerator for at least 30 minutes.

divide the prawns and scallops into separate groups. Thread the prawns and pineapple alternately on to 4 presoaked bamboo skewers (see below), leaving some space at either end. Thread the scallops and the remaining pineapple on to another 4 presoaked bamboo skewers.

cook the skewers under a preheated hot grill for 8–10 minutes, turning once, until the prawns and scallops are cooked through and tender. Serve hot.

Serves 4
Preparation time: *20 minutes, plus marinating*
Cooking time: *8–10 minutes*

clipboard: Use bamboo skewers 18–20 cm (7–8 inches) long and soak them in cold water for about 1 hour before you need them to help stop them burning during cooking.

Soups

Red Pork Noodle Soup

Chinese flowering cabbage, choi sum, is a member of the same family as pak choi. It has light green leaves, long stems and yellow flowers, and can be eaten on its own as a steamed vegetable or added to soups and stir-fries.

175 g (6 oz) fresh egg noodles

1 teaspoon Garlic Oil (see page 250)

2 choi sum, sliced

5 g (¼ oz) spring onion, finely sliced

1 tablespoon soy sauce

5 g (¼ oz) fresh coriander leaves

pinch of pepper

200 g (7 oz) Red Roast Pork, sliced (see page 122)

600 ml (1 pint) Chicken Stock (see page 14)

Dipping sauce

4 tablespoons distilled white vinegar

2–3 tablespoons nam pla (fish sauce)

1 large fresh red chilli, sliced

cook the noodles in a large saucepan of boiling water for 2–3 minutes, untangling them while they are boiling. Drain and mix in the garlic oil to prevent sticking.

meanwhile, cook the choi sum in a separate saucepan of boiling water for 1 minute, drain and reserve.

put the noodles in a large, heatproof serving bowl, then add the choi sum, spring onion, soy sauce, coriander leaves and pepper. Arrange the pork slices on the top. Heat the stock to boiling point and pour it over the pork, noodles and vegetables.

combine all the ingredients for the dipping sauce in a small bowl and serve with the soup.

Serves 4
Preparation time: *10 minutes*
Cooking time: *5 minutes*

Mussel Soup

Similar in appearance to glass (cellophane) noodles, rice vermicelli are used in salads and spring rolls as well as in soups, as here. They should always be soaked in hot water to soften them before use.

500 g (1 lb) live mussels

300 ml (½ pint) coconut milk

600 ml (1 pint) Fish Stock (see page 15)

75 g (3 oz) dried rice vermicelli, soaked in hot water for 15–20 minutes and drained

1 tablespoon peeled and finely chopped fresh root ginger

50 g (2 oz) fresh coriander stalks and roots

½ lemon grass stalk, chopped

2 small fresh red chillies, finely sliced

1 tablespoon nam pla (fish sauce)

1 tablespoon lime juice

25 g (1 oz) fresh coriander leaves, to garnish

wash the mussels in cold water and scrape away any barnacles with a sharp knife. Remove the beards, then leave the mussels to soak for about 1 hour in cold water. Drain and tap any open shells to make sure that they close. Discard any mussels that remain open.

put the mussels in a saucepan, cover and cook over a moderate heat, shaking the pan occasionally, for 3–4 minutes until they have opened. Discard any that remain closed. Remove the mussels with a slotted spoon and reserve.

add all the remaining ingredients to the pan and simmer for 15 minutes. Return the mussels to the pan and simmer for 1 minute. Serve hot, garnished with coriander leaves.

Serves 4
Preparation time: *20 minutes, plus soaking*
Cooking time: *20 minutes*

Glass Noodle Soup

Glass or cellophane noodles are also known as bean thread noodles or bean vermicelli. Soak them for about 15 minutes in hot water to soften before use.

125 g (4 oz) cucumber, roughly chopped

1 onion, halved

2 garlic cloves, halved

50 g (2 oz) white cabbage, chopped

600 ml (1 pint) water

125 g (4 oz) dried glass noodles, soaked for about 15 minutes in hot water and drained

25 g (1 oz) dried tofu sheets, soaked for 2–3 hours, drained and torn into pieces

15 g (½ oz) dried lily flowers, soaked and drained, or canned, drained bamboo shoots, thinly sliced

1 teaspoon salt

1 teaspoon palm sugar or light muscovado sugar

½ teaspoon soy sauce

2 large dried shiitake mushrooms, soaked in warm water for 15–20 minutes, drained and thinly sliced, hard stalks cut away and added to a stockpot

chopped celery leaves, to garnish

put the cucumber, onion, garlic and cabbage in a food processor and process for 15 seconds. Turn the mixture into a saucepan and add the measurement water. Bring to the boil, then reduce the heat and cook for 2 minutes, stirring occasionally.

strain the stock into a larger saucepan and add the noodles, tofu, lily flowers or bamboo shoots, salt, sugar and soy sauce. Stir well, then cook over a moderate heat for about 3 minutes. Taste and adjust the seasoning, if necessary.

pour the soup into a serving bowl, arrange the mushroom slices in the centre and sprinkle with chopped celery leaves. Serve immediately.

Serves 4
Preparation time: *10 minutes, plus soaking*
Cooking time: *about 5 minutes*

Khun Tom's Pumpkin Soup

1 teaspoon finely sliced lemon grass

1 teaspoon peeled and finely sliced fresh galangal

1 tablespoon basil leaves

½ green pepper, cored, deseeded and chopped

3 kaffir lime leaves

100 ml (3½ fl oz) water

1 tablespoon groundnut oil

2 garlic cloves, finely chopped

10 shallots, thinly sliced

1 teaspoon crushed dried chillies

1 small fresh red chilli, chopped

500 ml (17 fl oz) Vegetable Stock (see page 15)

50 g (2 oz) green beans, chopped

3 tablespoons vegetarian nam pla (fish sauce) or soy sauce

750 g (1½ lb) peeled and deseeded pumpkin, cubed

1 teaspoon palm sugar or light muscovado sugar

1 teaspoon ground white pepper

1 tablespoon Crushed Roasted Nuts (see page 248) or crunchy peanut butter

3 teaspoons curry powder

175 ml (6 fl oz) coconut milk

2 teaspoons cornflour

Crispy Basil (see page 248), to garnish

put the lemon grass, galangal, basil leaves, green pepper, lime leaves and measurement water in a food processor and process until blended, then strain and discard the water, reserving the purée.

heat the oil in a wok or large frying pan. Add the garlic, shallots and crushed dried and fresh chillies and stir-fry over a high heat for 1 minute.

add the purée, 400 ml (14 fl oz) of the stock, the green beans, nam pla or soy sauce and pumpkin and stir over a moderate heat. Add the sugar, pepper, nuts or peanut butter and curry powder and stir again. Cook, stirring frequently, for 10 minutes, or until the pumpkin is tender, then add the coconut milk, bring to the boil and boil hard for 1 minute.

blend the remaining stock with the cornflour to form a smooth paste, add to the soup and cook, stirring, until thickened.

ladle the soup into a large serving bowl, top with the crispy basil and serve immediately.

Serves 4
Preparation time: *30 minutes*
Cooking time: *15 minutes*

Banana Soup

The bananas used by Thai cooks tend to be smaller and sweeter than the ones normally found in Western supermarkets, but this savoury soup uses a single large banana.

1 tablespoon groundnut oil

50 g (2 oz) spring onions (including green shoots), sliced

25 g (1 oz) garlic, sliced

200 ml (7 fl oz) coconut milk

400 ml (14 fl oz) Vegetable Stock (see page 15)

¼ teaspoon ground white pepper

3 teaspoons vegetarian nam pla (fish sauce) or soy sauce

¼ teaspoon salt

½ teaspoon palm sugar or light muscovado sugar

1 large banana, peeled and diagonally cut into thin slices

1 large fresh red chilli, diagonally sliced

very fine strips of spring onion, to garnish

heat the oil in a wok or large frying pan over a moderately high heat and stir-fry the spring onions and garlic for 1–2 minutes. Add all the other ingredients and cook, stirring frequently, for 5 minutes.

if you prefer a blended soup, set aside about one-quarter of the banana and chilli slices, then purée the remainder with the soup in a food processor or blender until smooth. Return the blended mixture to the pan, add the reserved banana and chilli slices and warm through for 3 minutes.

serve immediately, garnished with very fine strips of spring onion.

Serves 4
Preparation time: *15 minutes*
Cooking time: *10 minutes*

Chicken and Coconut Milk Soup

600 ml (1 pint) Chicken Stock (see page 14)

6 kaffir lime leaves, torn, or ¼ teaspoon grated lime rind

1 lemon grass stalk, diagonally sliced, or ¼ teaspoon grated lemon rind

5 cm (2 inch) piece of fresh galangal or root ginger, peeled and finely sliced

200 ml (7 fl oz) coconut milk

8 tablespoons nam pla (fish sauce)

2 teaspoons palm sugar or light muscovado sugar

6 tablespoons lime juice

250 g (8 oz) boneless chicken, skinned and cut into small pieces

4 tablespoons chilli oil or 4 small fresh red chillies, finely sliced into rings (optional)

heat the stock in a saucepan over a moderate heat, then stir in the lime leaves or lime rind, lemon grass or lemon rind and galangal or ginger. As the stock is simmering, add the coconut milk, nam pla, sugar and lime juice. Stir well, then add the chicken and simmer for 5 minutes.

just before serving, add the chilli oil or chillies, if liked, stir again and serve immediately.

Serves 4
Preparation time: *6 minutes*
Cooking time: *10 minutes*

clipboard: To make coconut cream and milk, mix together 400 g (13 oz) grated fresh coconut or desiccated coconut and 900 ml (1½ pints) milk in a saucepan. Bring to the boil, then reduce the heat and simmer, stirring occasionally, until the mixture is reduced by one-third. Strain, pressing the mixture against the side of the sieve to extract as much liquid as possible. Pour the strained coconut milk into a bowl and chill in the refrigerator. When it is really cold, skim off the thicker 'cream' that rises to the surface. The remaining liquid is the coconut milk.

Prawn and Lime Soup

The roots of coriander are used in many Thai dishes, but only the refreshing leaves are added to this delicious soup, which can be served with rice.

750 g (1½ lb) raw prawns

2 litres (3½ pints) water

6 small kaffir lime leaves or ¼ teaspoon grated lime rind

1 tablespoon chopped lemon grass or ¼ teaspoon grated lemon rind

2 teaspoons nam pla (fish sauce)

75 ml (3 fl oz) lime juice

4 tablespoons fresh coriander leaves, chopped

3 tablespoons sliced spring onions

1 fresh red chilli, deseeded and sliced into 2.5 cm (1 inch) strips

salt and pepper (optional)

very fine strips of spring onion, to garnish

peel the prawns and remove the dark vein running along the back. Rinse under cold running water and pat dry with kitchen paper. Set aside while you make the soup.

pour the measurement water into a large saucepan and bring to the boil. Add the lime leaves or lime rind and lemon grass or lemon rind, reduce the heat and simmer for 10 minutes. Add the nam pla and cook for a further 5 minutes.

add the prawns and lime juice to the pan and cook over a low heat for a few minutes until the prawns have turned pink and are cooked through.

add the coriander, spring onions and chilli to the soup. Taste and adjust the seasoning, if necessary, and serve very hot in individual bowls, garnished with very fine strips of spring onion.

Serves 6
Preparation time: *15 minutes*
Cooking time: *20 minutes*

Rice Noodle Soup

Tofu is a white curd, derived from unfermented soya bean paste, and sometimes known as beancurd. You can buy pieces of soft tofu that have been deep-fried so that the outside has a brown crust and the centre is hard and dry.

750 ml (1¼ pints) Vegetable Stock (see page 15)

3 spring onions, cut into 2.5 cm (1 inch) lengths

2 baby corn cobs, diagonally sliced

1 tomato, finely diced

1 red onion, cut into slivers

6 kaffir lime leaves or ¼ teaspoon grated lime rind

1 celery stick, chopped

125 g (4 oz) ready-fried tofu, diced

1 tablespoon soy sauce

1 teaspoon pepper

1 heaped teaspoon crushed dried chillies

175 g (6 oz) dried wide rice noodles, soaked for about 15 minutes in hot water and drained

fresh coriander sprigs, to garnish

lime quarters, to serve (optional)

heat the stock in a saucepan over a moderate heat, then add all the remaining ingredients, except the noodles and a few of the red onion slivers, and stir well.

bring to the boil and boil for 30 seconds, then reduce the heat and simmer for 5 minutes. Add the noodles and simmer for a further 2 minutes.

pour into a serving bowl, garnish with coriander sprigs and the remaining red onion slivers and serve with lime quarters, if liked.

Serves 4
Preparation time: *10 minutes, plus soaking*
Cooking time: *10 minutes*

Clear Tofu Soup

Tofu is ideal for use in soups because it takes on the other flavours of the dish. This is a quick and easy soup to make.

1 litre (1¾ pints) Vegetable Stock (see page 15)

250 g (8 oz) minced pork

300 g (10 oz) firm tofu, cut into large squares

125 g (4 oz) fresh bean sprouts

4 tablespoons nam pla (fish sauce)

2 spring onions, finely chopped

1 celery stick with leaves, chopped

pepper

heat the stock in a saucepan over a moderate heat. Put the pork in a bowl, add about 250 ml (8 fl oz) of the hot stock and stir with a fork to break up the meat so that no lumps remain.

add the pork mixture to the stock in the pan and cook over a moderate heat for 5 minutes. Stir in the tofu, bean sprouts, nam pla, spring onions and celery and bring to the boil. Reduce the heat and simmer for a further 3 minutes.

transfer the soup to a serving bowl, season with pepper and serve on its own as a starter or as an accompaniment to the main meal, in the traditional Thai way.

Serves 4
Preparation time: *10 minutes*
Cooking time: *10 minutes*

clipboard: You can store fresh tofu in the refrigerator for up to 4 days. Cover it with water and make sure that you change the water every day.

Salads

Minced Fish Salad

Catfish is a notoriously bony fish, and you might find that you need to use tweezers to pick out all the little bones.

625 g (1¼ lb) whole catfish, cleaned

12 small fresh green chillies, finely sliced

½ red onion, finely sliced

15 g (½ oz) fresh coriander leaves, stalks and roots, finely chopped, plus extra leaves to garnish

3 tablespoons lime juice

3 tablespoons nam pla (fish sauce)

1½ tablespoons palm sugar or light muscovado sugar

¼ large, hard green mango, peeled and grated (optional)

40 g (1½ oz) Crushed Roasted Nuts (see page 248)

about 750 ml (1¼ pints) oil, for deep-frying

To garnish

shredded white cabbage

whole fresh red chillies

put the catfish in a foil-lined grill pan and cook under a preheated moderate grill for 30 minutes or until cooked and tender, turning the fish over halfway through the cooking time. Leave to cool.

skin the fish and remove the flesh, carefully discarding any bones. Mince the fish in a food processor or chop it very finely and set aside.

put all the remaining ingredients, except the oil, in a bowl and mix well to make a sauce.

heat the oil in a wok or deep frying pan to 180–190°C (350–375°F), or until a cube of bread browns in 30 seconds. Deep-fry the minced fish, in batches, for 4–5 minutes, stirring occasionally. Remove with a slotted spoon and drain on kitchen paper.

arrange the minced fish on a serving dish. Pour the sauce over the top of the fish and serve, garnished with shredded cabbage, coriander leaves and whole red chillies.

Serves 4
Preparation time: *15 minutes*
Cooking time: *45 minutes*

Deep-fried Dried Fish Salad

Mangoes can have green, yellow, red or purple flesh, but the green mangoes used here have a much tarter flavour than the larger, yellow-fleshed fruits used in desserts.

6 small fresh green and red chillies, finely sliced

½ red onion, finely chopped

15 g (½ oz) fresh coriander leaves, stalks and roots, finely chopped, plus extra leaves to garnish

2 tablespoons lime juice

½ tablespoon nam pla (fish sauce)

1½ tablespoons palm sugar or light muscovado sugar

¼ large, hard green mango, peeled and grated, plus extra matchsticks to garnish

about 750 ml (1¼ pints) oil, for deep-frying

50 g (2 oz) small dried fish

lettuce leaves, to serve

put the chillies and red onion in a mortar and pound with a pestle to a thick paste. Add the chopped coriander and pound again. Add the lime juice, nam pla, sugar and green mango and pound once more until the ingredients are thoroughly blended.

heat the oil in a wok or large frying pan to 180–190°C (350–375°F), or until a cube of bread browns in 30 seconds. Deep-fry the dried fish, in batches, for 2–3 minutes until golden and crisp. Remove with a slotted spoon and drain on kitchen paper.

arrange some lettuce leaves on a serving dish and place the fish on top. Pour over the sauce from the mortar, garnish with coriander leaves and serve immediately.

Serves 4
Preparation time: *10–15 minutes*
Cooking time: *5 minutes*

Glass Noodle Salad

Glass or cellophane noodles are often sold dried in bundles.

Do not oversoak or they will disintegrate when cooked.

200 g (7 oz) dried glass noodles, soaked for about 15 minutes in hot water and drained

1 tomato, halved and sliced

20 g (¾ oz) celery stick, chopped

20 g (¾ oz) spring onion, chopped

1 onion, halved and sliced

50 g (2 oz) green pepper, cored, deseeded and chopped

juice of 2 limes

5 small fresh green chillies, finely chopped

2 teaspoons palm sugar or light muscovado sugar

50 g (2 oz) Crushed Roasted Nuts – use peanuts (see page 248)

1 teaspoon crushed dried chillies

½ teaspoon salt

2½ tablespoons vegetarian nam pla (fish sauce) or soy sauce

fresh coriander sprigs, to garnish

cook the noodles in a saucepan of boiling water for 3–4 minutes. Drain and rinse under cold running water to prevent further cooking.

cut the noodles into pieces about 12 cm (5 inches) long. Put them in a large serving bowl, add all the remaining ingredients and mix thoroughly for 2 minutes.

serve the salad at room temperature, garnished with coriander sprigs.

Serves 4
Preparation time: *15 minutes, plus soaking*
Cooking time: *3–5 minutes*

Cucumber Salad with Roasted Cashews

Thai cooks peel a cucumber by holding it flat and chopping it lengthways with a large knife and a quick motion, turning the cucumber as they go. They scrape off the long strips, then continue until they reach the seeds, which they discard.

1 cucumber

2 teaspoons palm sugar or light muscovado sugar

1½ teaspoons vegetarian nam pla (fish sauce) or soy sauce

100 g (3½ oz) Crushed Roasted Nuts – use cashew nuts (see page 248)

1 teaspoon crushed dried chillies

juice of 2 limes

½ teaspoon salt

peel the cucumber and chop it into long strips, discarding the seeds.

put the cucumber in a large serving bowl, add all the remaining ingredients and toss together until thoroughly mixed.

serve the salad at room temperature.

Serves 4
Preparation time: *10 minutes*

Pomelo Salad

This refreshing salad could not be easier to make.
If you cannot find pomelos, use grapefruit, which they
closely resemble.

½ pomelo or 1 grapefruit

4 shallots, sliced

½ teaspoon crushed dried chillies

2 tablespoons palm sugar or light muscovado sugar

2 tablespoons vegetarian nam pla (fish sauce) or soy sauce

juice of 2 limes

¼ teaspoon salt

holding the fruit over a bowl, remove the membranes and separate and halve the segments. Discard the skin.

add all the remaining ingredients to the bowl and mix thoroughly. Serve the salad at room temperature.

Serves 4
Preparation time: *5 minutes*

clipboard: Pomelos, which are sometimes known as pummelos or shaddocks, are the largest of the citrus fruits, at about 30 cm (12 inches) across. They are widely used in Southeast Asia and are one of the antecedents of the grapefruit, although they are sweeter than that fruit.

Green Bean Salad

Use peanuts rather than cashew nuts in this recipe for an authentic combination. Treat the soft tofu carefully because it will quickly lose its shape when it is handled.

50 g (2 oz) runner beans or French beans, thinly sliced

100 g (3½ oz) silken tofu

100 ml (3½ fl oz) coconut milk

1 shallot, sliced

25 g (1 oz) Crushed Roasted Nuts – use peanuts (see page 248)

1 teaspoon crushed dried chillies

1 tablespoon lime juice

1 teaspoon palm sugar or light muscovado sugar

2 tablespoons soy sauce

1 teaspoon salt

cook the beans in a saucepan of boiling water for 2 minutes. Drain and set aside.

soften the tofu in the coconut milk in a saucepan over a low heat until it has partially melted. Remove the pan from the heat and add the beans and all the remaining ingredients.

stir the ingredients thoroughly to combine, then turn them out on to a serving dish. Serve the salad at room temperature.

Serves 6
Preparation time: *10 minutes*
Cooking time: *5–6 minutes*

Curried Vegetable Salad

2 celery sticks, roughly chopped

4 carrots, thinly sliced

125 g (4 oz) cabbage, finely sliced

125 g (4 oz) thin green beans

½ red pepper, cored, deseeded and diced

½ green pepper, cored, deseeded and diced

250 g (8 oz) fresh bean sprouts

200 g (7 oz) canned, drained water chestnuts, sliced

Curry dressing

125 g (4 oz) creamed coconut

150 ml (¼ pint) water

2 tablespoons groundnut oil

2 tablespoons Red Curry Paste (see page 12)

2 tablespoons dark soy sauce

2 tablespoons lime juice

2 teaspoons palm sugar or light muscovado sugar

¼ teaspoon salt

1 teaspoon ground coriander

2 teaspoons ground cumin

3 tablespoons Crushed Roasted Nuts
(see page 248)

To garnish

slivers of fresh coconut

mint sprigs (optional)

cook all the vegetables, except the bean sprouts and water chestnuts, in a large saucepan of boiling water for 3–4 minutes. They should retain their fresh colour and be slightly tender but still crisp. Drain and mix in a bowl with the bean sprouts and water chestnuts.

make the curry dressing. Put the creamed coconut in a separate bowl and cover with the measurement water. Stir well until the creamed coconut has completely dissolved, then set aside.

heat the oil in a wok or frying pan over a low heat and stir-fry the curry paste for 1–2 minutes. Add the creamed coconut, soy sauce, lime juice, sugar, salt, coriander, cumin and nuts. Stir well and heat through gently for 3–4 minutes. Pour the dressing over the vegetables and toss gently.

transfer the vegetables to a serving dish and serve warm, garnished with slivers of coconut, and mint sprigs, if liked.

Serves 4–6
Preparation time: *25 minutes*
Cooking time: *7–10 minutes*

Chicken and Papaya Salad

Papaya is often cooked and served with poultry or meat in Thailand as a cooling contrast to a spicy dressing. If papayas are difficult to obtain, use mango, pineapple or melon instead.

Dressing

2 small fresh green or red chillies, deseeded and chopped

2 large garlic cloves, chopped

finely grated rind of 1 lime

6 tablespoons lime juice

2–3 tablespoons nam pla (fish sauce)

2–3 tablespoons palm sugar or light muscovado sugar, to taste

Salad

500 g (1 lb) chicken breast fillets, skinned

corn or groundnut oil, for brushing

2 ripe papayas

1 crisp lettuce, such as iceberg, leaves separated

½ large cucumber, thinly sliced

75 g (3 oz) fresh bean sprouts

make the dressing. Put the chillies, garlic and lime rind in a mortar and pound with a pestle to a paste.

stir in the lime juice and nam pla until evenly mixed with the chilli and garlic paste, then add the sugar to taste. Cover and set aside while you prepare the salad ingredients and cook the chicken.

brush the chicken breasts liberally with oil. Cook under a preheated hot grill for about 7 minutes on each side, or until cooked through.

peel the papayas and cut each one in half lengthways. Scoop out and discard the seeds and slice the flesh thinly.

arrange the lettuce leaves around the edge of a serving dish, then place the papaya, cucumber and bean sprouts attractively on top.

place the chicken on a board. With a very sharp knife, cut it diagonally into bite-sized slices. Arrange the chicken on top of the salad and sprinkle over the dressing. Leave the salad to stand for a few minutes before serving.

Serves 4
Preparation time: *30 minutes*
Cooking time: *15 minutes*

Sweet and Sour Salad

Remember to handle chillies with care. Wear gloves if your hands are sensitive, and be careful not to touch any part of your face, particularly your eyes, before you have washed your hands.

1 large garlic clove, chopped

2 fresh red bird's eye chillies, chopped

125 g (4 oz) carrots, thinly sliced

125 g (4 oz) white cabbage, thinly sliced

2 green beans, cut into 2.5 cm (1 inch) lengths

2 tomatoes, chopped

1½ tablespoons nam pla (fish sauce)

3 tablespoons lemon juice

3 tablespoons palm sugar or light muscovado sugar

1 tablespoon ground dried shrimp

2 tablespoons Crushed Roasted Nuts (see page 248)

1 frisée lettuce, separated into leaves, to serve

basil sprigs, to garnish

put the garlic and chillies in a food processor and process to a thick paste. Alternatively, put them in a mortar and pound with a pestle.

transfer the mixture to a bowl, add the carrots, cabbage, green beans, tomatoes, nam pla, lemon juice, sugar, ground dried shrimp and nuts and mix well so that all the ingredients are thoroughly blended.

arrange a bed of lettuce in a shallow serving dish, top with the salad, garnish with basil sprigs and serve.

Serves 4
Preparation time: *15 minutes*

Green Mango Salad

Like papayas, mangoes are eaten ripe and unripe. The tart flavour of green mangoes can be bitter, and you might want to add a little more sugar to this refreshing salad.

I large, hard green mango, peeled, stoned and grated

I red onion, chopped, plus extra slivers to garnish

30 g (1¼ oz) palm sugar or light muscovado sugar

I tablespoon lime juice

I tablespoon soy sauce

½ teaspoon salt

I teaspoon crushed dried chillies

50 g (2 oz) Crushed Roasted Nuts (see page 248)

To garnish

fresh coriander leaves, finely chopped

I fresh red chilli, roughly chopped

stir together the mango and red onion in a large bowl. Add the sugar, lime juice, soy sauce, salt and crushed dried chillies and stir thoroughly for 1–2 minutes.

add the nuts, give the salad a final stir and turn out on to a serving dish.

garnish the salad with chopped coriander and red chilli and slivers of red onion before serving.

Serves 3–4
Preparation time: *15 minutes*

Green Papaya Salad

Small bird's eye chillies have given Thai cooking its reputation for being hot. They are often used whole because cutting them up can make them even hotter.

375 g (12 oz) green papayas, peeled and deseeded

2 garlic cloves, crushed

3 fresh red bird's eye chillies, chopped, plus extra whole chillies to garnish

4 cherry tomatoes

2 tablespoons nam pla (fish sauce)

2 teaspoons caster sugar

juice of 1 lime

1 tablespoon dried shrimp paste

3 tablespoons roasted peanuts, chopped

2 tablespoons roughly chopped fresh coriander leaves, plus extra leaves to garnish

roughly grate the papaya flesh or cut it into fine shreds.

put the garlic, chillies and cherry tomatoes in a mortar and pound with a pestle to a rough purée.

add the grated papaya, nam pla, sugar, lime juice and shrimp paste and pound together until roughly mixed.

add the chopped peanuts and coriander and serve, garnished with the whole chillies and coriander leaves.

Serves 4
Preparation time: *10 minutes*

clipboard: Some people are sensitive to the sap of green papayas, so wear disposable gloves the first time you handle this fruit. When it is grown in the tropics, the papaya tree bears fruit all year round, making it an important source of fruit.

Vegetables

Stir-fried Vegetables with Cashew Nuts

Make sure that all the vegetable pieces are more or less the same size so that they cook evenly and equally. Take care not to overcook them – the vegetables should have a definite 'bite'.

50 g (2 oz) unroasted, unsalted cashew nuts

250 g (8 oz) Chinese leaves, chopped into 2.5 cm (1 inch) pieces

50 g (2 oz) cauliflower florets

50 g (2 oz) broccoli, separated into florets

50 g (2 oz) white cabbage, chopped

2 baby corn cobs, diagonally sliced

1 tomato, cut into 8 pieces

5 garlic cloves, chopped

1½ tablespoons soy sauce

1 teaspoon palm sugar or light muscovado sugar

100 ml (3½ fl oz) water

2½ tablespoons groundnut oil

pepper (optional)

dry-fry the nuts in a frying pan, using no oil, stirring constantly until golden brown. Remove from the heat and leave to cool.

put the nuts and all the remaining ingredients, except the oil and pepper, in a bowl and mix thoroughly.

heat the oil in a wok or large frying pan over a high heat and stir-fry the contents of the bowl for 2–3 minutes. Taste and season with pepper, if necessary. Serve immediately.

Serves 3–4
Preparation time: *25 minutes*
Cooking time: *5–8 minutes*

Vegetables with Oyster Sauce

Vegetarians can use soy sauce in this recipe instead of oyster sauce, although it will not have the distinctive flavour of the fish-based sauce.

3 tablespoons vegetable oil

1 garlic clove, crushed

125 g (4 oz) cabbage, shredded

125 g (4 oz) cauliflower florets

½ teaspoon pepper

2 tablespoons oyster sauce

150 ml (¼ pint) Chicken or Vegetable Stock
(see pages 14–15)

125 g (4 oz) broccoli florets

2 carrots, cut into fine strips, plus extra shredded carrot to garnish

125 g (4 oz) mushrooms, thinly sliced

1 onion, sliced into rings

50 g (2 oz) fresh bean sprouts

boiled rice, to serve

heat the oil in a wok or large frying pan over a moderate heat and stir-fry the garlic for 1 minute, or until golden. Do not allow it to get too brown.

add the cabbage, cauliflower and pepper, then stir in the oyster sauce and stock. Cook, stirring constantly, for 3 minutes.

add the broccoli, carrots, mushrooms, onion and bean sprouts and stir-fry for 2 minutes.

transfer the fried vegetables to a large warm dish or platter, garnish with shredded carrot and serve immediately with boiled rice.

Serves 4
Preparation time: *15 minutes*
Cooking time: *6–7 minutes*

Mushroom and Mangetout Stir-fry

Shiitake mushrooms can be found dried in oriental food stores, health food stores and some supermarkets, which also sometimes sell them fresh.

10 dried shiitake mushrooms

1 tablespoon groundnut oil

2 large garlic cloves, chopped

125 g (4 oz) baby corn cobs, diagonally sliced

125 g (4 oz) drained, canned bamboo shoots

50 g (2 oz) mangetout

1 teaspoon palm sugar or light muscovado sugar

3 tablespoons soy sauce

1 tablespoon water

pepper

to garnish

small green chillies

basil sprigs

soak the mushrooms in warm water for 15–20 minutes, then drain and slice. (The hard stalks should be cut away and added to a stockpot.)

heat the oil in a wok or large frying pan over a high heat and briefly stir-fry the garlic, then add all the remaining ingredients, in turn, adding the mushrooms just before the bamboo shoots.

stir-fry the vegetables for 2–3 minutes, then turn out on to a serving dish. Garnish with green chillies and basil sprigs and serve immediately.

Serves 4
Preparation time: *10 minutes, plus soaking*
Cooking time: *3–4 minutes*

Stuffed Omelette

This is a popular lunchtime dish, often prepared and sold by roadside and market stalls.

about 1 tablespoon groundnut oil

3 eggs, beaten

salt and pepper

Crispy Basil (see page 248), to garnish

Filling

3 tablespoons groundnut oil

2 garlic cloves, chopped

1 onion, finely chopped

2 tablespoons chopped green beans

2 tablespoons chopped asparagus

3 baby corn cobs, thinly sliced

1 tomato, diced

4 dried shiitake mushrooms, soaked for 15–20 minutes in warm water, drained and sliced, hard stalks cut away and added to a stockpot

1½ teaspoons palm sugar or light muscovado sugar

2 teaspoons soy sauce

50 ml (2 fl oz) water

pinch of salt

make the filling. Heat the oil in a wok or large frying pan over a moderately high heat and stir-fry the garlic and onion for 30 seconds. Add the green beans, asparagus, baby corn, tomato, mushrooms, sugar and soy sauce and stir-fry for 3–4 minutes. Add the measurement water and salt and stir-fry for a further 2 minutes. Remove the mixture from the pan and set aside. Wipe the pan clean with kitchen paper.

make the omelette. Heat the oil in the pan, making sure that it coats not only the base of the pan but as much of the side as possible. Pour off any excess. Pour in the eggs and swirl them around in the pan to form a large, thin omelette. Loosen the omelette and move it around with a spatula to make sure that it is not sticking to the pan, adding a little more oil if necessary.

when the omelette is almost firm, put the filling in the centre and fold both sides and ends over to form an oblong parcel, constantly making sure that the omelette is not sticking underneath.

carefully remove the omelette from the pan and place it in a serving dish. Serve immediately, garnished with crispy basil.

Serves 1–2
Preparation time: *8–10 minutes, plus soaking*
Cooking time: *8–10 minutes*

Thai Dining

Thai people love snacking, and they often stop at market stalls several times a day to enjoy freshly cooked food. Meals eaten at home and in restaurants are taken in the same informal way. There are no distinct courses to a Thai meal, as there are in Western ones. Instead, a variety of dishes is presented at the same time, but each dish is carefully chosen in relation to the others, to provide a harmonious blend of flavours, textures and cooking styles.

A Thai meal generally consists of a number of different dishes, plus a large bowl of rice. There might be a soup, served in a large bowl, which everyone can dip into, or in small individual bowls; a curry; something steamed or fried; a salad; some dipping sauces and pickles; and fresh fruit to finish the meal. All these dishes will appear on the table at the same time. Diners put a mound of rice on their plates, followed by a little of one of the other dishes. Thais do not put everything on their plates at once and eat it all together, as people do in the West. They like to appreciate all the different tastes and textures separately.

Thais use their fingers or a fork and spoon, unless they are eating noodles, when chopsticks, a sign of Chinese influence on Thai cuisine, are used.

You will not usually find a dessert on the menu, other than fruit, unless it is a special occasion. There are, however, a large number of Thai sweet dishes or sweetmeats, and a great many of them involve egg yolks and sugar, which is an indication of the Portuguese influence in this part of the world. Some take a long time to make and involve a number of different stages.

Menu planning

When you are planning a menu, keep the following points in mind and you will easily make some memorable meals.

Soups are popular dishes in Thailand. Often fiercely hot, they may be the only dish at a meal, especially in the middle of the day. However, it has become more usual for Thai restaurants, especially in the West, to serve a soup as the first course in a meal.

From traditional egg noodles to delicately flavoured rice vermicelli, noodles often provide the basis of a Thai meal.

If you do not begin your meal with soup, a choice of two or three of the starters in this book will make an appetizing light opening course for a Thai meal. Few Thais would object to this approach – after all, many of them buy their snacks two or three at a time from street vendors' stalls.

For the main part of the meal, be careful to choose dishes that work well together. A fiery meat or poultry curry could overpower a more delicate fish dish, for example. On the other hand, a fiery curry needs something cooling, like a simple rice dish or a fresh green salad, to complement and counteract the stronger flavours.

Do not serve dishes that have all been cooked in the same way – four stir-fries would all tend to have the same texture. Instead, plan for a variety of cooking styles, such as a stir-fry, a steamed dish and, perhaps, something deep-fried. Similarly, try to vary the main ingredients, so that you have a meat dish, a fish dish and a vegetable dish.

Thais, like most Asians, are not great dessert eaters. If you do not want to serve one of the desserts in this book, it is perfectly acceptable to serve a bowl of fresh fruits in season.

Creating a balance of different textures, colours and fiery and cool or bland flavours is the key to a successful Thai meal.

Rice and noodles

Rice and noodles provide the perfect accompaniment to more strongly flavoured dishes. However, it is probably better to serve one or other of these at a meal, not both.

Thailand is not the largest rice producer in the world, but it is generally considered to produce the best quality rice, and the dual aspects of quality and quantity have led to it becoming the world's largest exporter of rice. Thai fragrant or jasmine rice is more expensive to buy than other long-grain rice, but it is so delicious that it is well worth paying extra for it, and Thai meals usually have a large bowl of hot jasmine rice at the centre.

Sticky or glutinous rice is often eaten with the fingers and formed into small balls, which are dipped into savoury dishes, especially in the north of Thailand. It is also the basis of several desserts (see page 230).

Noodles can be made of rice, mung bean or wheat flour and egg, and they can be almost any length and thickness. They are available fresh and dried (see page 18).

Coconut cream and milk

Thai curries get much of their creaminess from coconut milk and cream, which is not the watery liquid found inside whole coconuts. Canned coconut milk is available, but you will get far better results if you make your own. A simple method of making coconut milk and cream is given on page 16.

Thai Fried Pies

250 g (8 oz) plain flour

½ teaspoon salt

125 g (4 oz) hard vegetable fat

2 tablespoons cold waterabout 750 ml (1¼ pints) groundnut oil, for deep-frying

Hot Sweet Sauce (see page 246), to serve

Filling

500 g (1 lb) pumpkin, peeled, deseeded and cut into chunks

250 ml (8 fl oz) coconut milk

1 tablespoon vegetarian nam pla (fish sauce) or soy sauce

1 lemon grass stalk, thinly sliced

1 kaffir lime leaf, torn

1 teaspoon crushed dried chillies

1 teaspoon Red Curry Paste (see page 12)

½ red pepper, cored, deseeded and diced

½ onion, finely chopped

3 tablespoons finely diced cooked carrot

3 tablespoons finely diced canned water chestnuts

make the filling. Put the pumpkin, coconut milk, nam pla or soy sauce, lemon grass, lime leaf and crushed dried chillies in a saucepan and bring to the boil. Reduce the heat and simmer for about 15 minutes, or until the pumpkin is tender. Mash the mixture in the pan and continue to simmer if you think it is too thin – it should be fairly thick. Remove from the heat and leave to cool.

meanwhile, make the pastry. Sift the flour and salt into a bowl. Cut the fat into small pieces and add to the flour, a little at a time, rubbing it in with your fingertips until the mixture resembles fine breadcrumbs. Add the measurement water and stir with a knife until it is incorporated. Knead the mixture quickly until a dough is formed, then wrap in foil and chill in the refrigerator for 10–15 minutes.

add the remaining filling ingredients to the cold pumpkin mixture and mix together.

roll out the chilled dough thinly, and cut it into 16 rounds, each 7 cm (3 inches) across. Divide the filling equally between the pastry rounds, fold over to enclose and seal with a fork.

heat the oil for in a wok or deep frying pan to 180–190°C (350–375°F), or until a cube of bread browns in 30 seconds. Deep-fry the pies, in 2 batches, for 5–6 minutes until golden brown. Remove with a slotted spoon and drain on kitchen paper.

serve the pies hot or warm, with the hot sweet sauce in a separate bowl.

Makes 16
Preparation time: *about 40 minutes, plus chilling*
Cooking time: *35–40 minutes*

Forest Curry with Lychees

Canned lychees are widely available, so even if you cannot find fresh ones, you can still make this curry. You can also use rambutans instead of lychees.

600 ml (1 pint) water

1 tablespoon Red Curry Paste (see page 12)

20 fresh lychees, stoned, or 500 g (1 lb) can lychees, drained and juice reserved

1¼ teaspoons salt

4 small round aubergines, quartered

50 g (2 oz) green beans, chopped into 2.5 cm (1 inch) lengths

6 kaffir lime leaves, torn

20 g (¾ oz) krachai or fresh galangal, peeled and sliced

4 baby corn cobs

15 g (½ oz) green peppercorns

2 large fresh green chillies

2 teaspoons palm sugar or light muscovado sugar

20 g (¾ oz) cucumber, diced

heat the measurement water in a saucepan, add the curry paste and stir to blend thoroughly. If you are using canned lychees, add the reserved juice now, then add the salt and bring the mixture to the boil, stirring.

reduce the heat to a slow boil and add all the remaining ingredients, except the lychees and cucumber. Cook, stirring, for 30 seconds.

add the lychees and cucumber and cook, stirring occasionally, for 3–4 minutes. Serve immediately.

Serves 4
Preparation time: *10 minutes*
Cooking time: *about 8 minutes*

clipboard: Krachai, which has a stronger flavour than galangal and ginger, is more often available dried in packets, but you may come across the fresh root in some oriental food stores.

Green Curry with Straw Mushrooms

Green curry paste is made from crushed fresh green chillies and herbs, and it is usually hot. Although you can buy canned and bottled pastes, it is easy to make your own.

300 ml (½ pint) coconut milk

40 g (1½ oz) Green Curry Paste (see page 13)

300 ml (½ pint) Vegetable Stock (see page 15)

4 small round aubergines, each cut into 8 pieces

40 g (1½ oz) palm sugar or light muscovado sugar

1 teaspoon salt

4 teaspoons vegetarian nam pla (fish sauce) or soy sauce

25 g (1 oz) krachai or fresh galangal, peeled and sliced

425 g (14 oz) can straw mushrooms, drained

50 g (2 oz) green pepper, cored, deseeded and thinly sliced

To garnish

handful of fresh basil leaves

2 tablespoons coconut milk

heat the coconut milk in a saucepan, add the curry paste and stir to blend thoroughly. Add the stock and then the aubergines, sugar, salt, nam pla or soy sauce, krachai or galangal and mushrooms. Bring to the boil and cook, stirring, for 2 minutes. Add the green pepper, reduce the heat and cook for 1 minute.

serve in a bowl, garnished with the basil leaves and drizzled with the coconut milk.

Serves 4
Preparation time: *7 minutes*
Cooking time: *8 minutes*

clipboard: Asian aubergines can be either long, thin and pink, small, round and pale green or tiny, round and darker green. They are often available in large supermarkets and Asian and oriental food stores. If you substitute the large purple-black variety more commonly found in Western stores, remember that they cook faster than the Asian types, so adjust your cooking times accordingly.

Yellow Curry with Carrots

150 ml (¼ pint) Vegetable Stock (see page 15)

5 kaffir lime leaves

25 g (1 oz) fresh galangal, peeled and sliced

175 g (6 oz) carrots, cut into chunks

4 garlic cloves, crushed

2 large fresh chillies (red and green)

1 tablespoon groundnut oil

2 tablespoons Crushed Roasted Nuts (see page 248)

300 ml (½ pint) coconut milk

2 tablespoons Yellow Curry Paste (see page 13)

8 canned, drained straw mushrooms

4 shallots

½ teaspoon salt, or to taste

put the stock in a saucepan, add the lime leaves, galangal, carrots, half the garlic and the whole chillies and simmer gently for 15 minutes. Strain the stock, reserving the liquid and both the carrots and chillies separately.

heat the oil in a wok or large frying pan and stir-fry the remaining garlic over a moderate heat for 1 minute. Add the reserved carrots and the nuts and stir-fry for 1 minute. Add the coconut milk and curry paste and stir until well blended. Add the reserved liquid and the whole mushrooms and shallots and simmer, stirring occasionally, for 15 minutes, or until the shallots are tender. Add the salt.

deseed and finely slice the reserved cooked chillies. Serve the curry garnished with the sliced chillies.

Serves 4
Preparation time: *15 minutes*
Cooking time: *35–40 minutes*

clipboard: Turmeric, which gives yellow curry paste its vibrant colour, comes from a rhizome, which has to be pounded or grated before it can be used. The dried ground form is an acceptable substitute for fresh turmeric – 2 teaspoons ground turmeric and 1 teaspoon palm sugar is the equivalent of 20 g (¾ oz) freshly grated turmeric.

Pork and Beef

Pork with Salted Eggs and Bean Sprouts

Salted eggs take a couple of weeks to prepare, so this is not a dish to make on the spur of the moment! It would make a filling dish for a supper party.

600 ml (1 pint) water

50 g (2 oz) salt

2 eggs

2 tablespoons vegetable oil

1 garlic clove, chopped

75 g (3 oz) minced pork

1 tablespoon oyster sauce

1 teaspoon palm sugar or light muscovado sugar

4 tablespoons Chicken Stock (see page 14)

1 tablespoon nam pla (fish sauce)

200 g (7 oz) fresh bean sprouts

2 large fresh red chillies, diagonally sliced

1 spring onion, diagonally sliced

fresh coriander leaves, to garnish

heat the measurement water in a saucepan over a moderate heat, add the salt and stir until it dissolves. Remove it from the heat and leave to cool. When it is cool, pour it into a jar and gently add the whole eggs. Put the lid on and leave to stand at room temperature for 15 days. Remove the eggs from the jar and hard-boil. Leave to cool, then shell and halve.

heat the oil in a wok or large frying pan and stir-fry the garlic and pork over a moderately high heat for 3 minutes. Add the oyster sauce, sugar, stock and nam pla and stir-fry for 5 minutes.

add the salted eggs and all the remaining ingredients and cook, stirring, for about 1 minute. Transfer to a serving dish, garnish with coriander leaves and serve immediately.

Serves 4
Preparation time: *30 minutes, plus cooling and standing*
Cooking time: *20 minutes*

Red Roast Pork

The red coloration from the marinade soaks into the edges of the pork, giving an attractive appearance to this dish.

750 g (1½ lb) pork shoulder, spare rib joint or leg, boned and rolled, fat removed

Marinade

50 g (2 oz) or 1 packet red roast pork seasoning mix

1 tablespoon tomato purée

2 tablespoons palm sugar or light muscovado sugar

1 tablespoon Chicken Stock (see page 14)

To garnish

fresh coriander leaves

fresh red chillies

make the marinade. Mix all the marinade ingredients together in a bowl. Cut the pork into 4 large pieces, add them to the marinade and turn in the marinade to coat thoroughly. Cover and leave to marinate in the refrigerator for at least 5 hours, preferably overnight.

put the pork in a roasting tin and roast in a preheated oven, 200°C (400°F), Gas Mark 6, for 1–1¼ hours, turning occasionally.

slice the pork thinly, arrange it on a serving dish and serve, garnished with coriander leaves and red chillies.

Serves 4
Preparation time: *10–15 minutes, plus marinating*
Cooking time: *1–1¼ hours*

Pork Satay

You can use oiled metal skewers for this satay or, more traditionally, bamboo skewers, which should be soaked in water for at least an hour before they are needed to help stop them splintering and scorching.

500 g (1 lb) pork fillet

1 teaspoon salt

2 teaspoons palm sugar or light muscovado sugar

1 teaspoon ground turmeric

1 teaspoon ground coriander

1 teaspoon ground cumin

175 ml (6 fl oz) coconut milk

chilli powder, for sprinkling

fresh coriander sprigs, to garnish

lemon slices, to serve

Peanut sauce

50 g (2 oz) unsalted peanuts, dry-fried

1 teaspoon salt

300 ml (½ pint) coconut milk

2 teaspoons Red Curry Paste (see page 12)

2 tablespoons palm sugar or light muscovado sugar

½ teaspoon lemon juice

cut the pork into 5 cm (2 inch) strips and put it in a large bowl. Add the salt, sugar, turmeric, ground coriander, cumin and 4 tablespoons of the coconut milk. Mix thoroughly, using your hands to knead the spices into the meat. Cover and leave to marinate in the refrigerator for at least 2 hours.

make the sauce. Put the peanuts and salt in a mortar and grind with a pestle to a thick cream. Set aside. Put half the remaining coconut milk in a saucepan with the curry paste. Heat gently for 3 minutes, stirring constantly. Stir in the ground peanuts with the sugar, lemon juice and the remaining coconut milk. Simmer gently for 20–30 minutes, stirring frequently to prevent the sauce from sticking. Transfer to a serving bowl.

thread the marinated pork on to skewers and cook on a barbecue or under a preheated hot grill for 12–15 minutes, turning them several times and brushing frequently with the marinade. Sprinkle the skewers with chilli powder, garnish with coriander sprigs and serve with the peanut sauce and some lemon slices.

Serves 4
Preparation time: *15–20 minutes, plus marinating*
Cooking time: *about 45 minutes*

Pork with Hot Sauces

375 g (12 oz) pork fillet

½ teaspoon salt

¼ teaspoon ground white pepper

15 g (½ oz) butter

1 tablespoon vegetable oil

3 garlic cloves

1 cm (½ inch) piece of fresh root ginger, peeled and chopped

2 fresh red chillies, chopped

1½ teaspoons ground cumin

½ cucumber, finely diced, to serve

Chilli and ginger sauce

2 fresh red chillies

2.5 cm (1 inch) piece of fresh root ginger, peeled and chopped

½ onion, grated

salt

Tomato and chilli sauce

2 tomatoes, skinned and chopped

2 garlic cloves, crushed

pinch of palm sugar or light muscovado sugar

1 teaspoon hot chilli powder

salt

slice the pork thinly and rub with the salt and pepper. Heat the butter and oil in a wok or large frying pan and stir-fry the pork over a moderate heat until lightly browned. Remove from the pan and keep warm.

chop the garlic finely and add to the pan with the ginger, chillies and cumin. Stir-fry for 2 minutes, then return the pork to the pan. Stir-fry for 2 minutes over a low heat, or until the meat is cooked through and tender. If necessary, add a sprinkling of water to keep the meat moist.

make the chilli and ginger sauce. Put all the sauce ingredients in a mortar and pound with a pestle to a smooth paste.

make the tomato and chilli sauce. Mix all the sauce ingredients together in a small bowl and season with salt to taste.

serve the stir-fried pork with the cucumber and the 2 hot sauces.

Serves 4
Preparation time: *15 minutes*
Cooking time: *8–10 minutes*

Grilled Beef with Spicy Sauce

This dish is from the north of Thailand, an area known as Issan. The food from here is greatly influenced by Laotian cuisine.

300 g (10 oz) sirloin steak

Spicy sauce

½ tomato, finely chopped

¼ red onion, finely chopped

1 tablespoon ground chilli

6 tablespoons nam pla (fish sauce)

2 tablespoons lime juice or tamarind water (see page 32)

2 teaspoons palm sugar or light muscovado sugar

1 teaspoon Ground Roast Rice (see page 248)

1 tablespoon Chicken Stock (see page 14)

To garnish

basil sprigs

flat leaf parsley sprigs

fresh coriander leaves

fresh red and green chillies

put the steak under a preheated hot grill and cook, turning it once, according to your taste.

while the meat is cooking, make the sauce. Mix all the sauce ingredients together in a bowl.

when the beef is ready, slice it up, arrange the pieces on a serving dish and garnish with the basil and parsley sprigs, coriander leaves and chillies. Serve the sauce separately.

Serves 4
Preparation time: *10 minutes*
Cooking time: *6 minutes (for medium-rare)*

clipboard: If you cannot find Thai or holy basil to use in Thai cooking, it is fine to use ordinary (European) basil, which has a sweeter flavour.

Thai Green Beef Curry

This green curry dish is typical of the cuisine of the central plains. Pork, chicken or duck can be used instead of beef.

2 tablespoons groundnut oil

2.5 cm (1 inch) piece of fresh root ginger, peeled and finely chopped

2 shallots, chopped

4 tablespoons Green Curry Paste (see page 13)

500 g (1 lb) fillet of beef, cubed

300 ml (½ pint) coconut milk

4 tablespoons nam pla (fish sauce)

1 teaspoon palm sugar or light muscovado sugar

3 kaffir lime leaves, finely chopped, or ¼ teaspoon grated lime rind

2 teaspoons tamarind water (see page 32)

1 fresh green chilli, deseeded and finely sliced

salt and pepper

boiled rice, to serve

To garnish

1 yellow pepper, cored, deseeded and cut into strips

fried chopped garlic (optional)

fresh red chilli, deseeded, cut into very fine strips and curled (optional – see page 148)

heat the oil in a wok or large frying pan and stir-fry the ginger and shallots over a low heat for about 3 minutes, or until softened. Add the curry paste and stir-fry for 2 minutes.

add the beef to the pan, stir until it is evenly coated in the spice mixture and stir-fry for 3 minutes to seal the meat. Stir in the coconut milk and bring it to the boil. Reduce the heat and cook the curry over a low heat, stirring occasionally, for about 10 minutes, or until the meat is cooked through and the sauce has thickened.

stir in the nam pla, sugar, lime leaves or lime rind, tamarind water and chilli. Cook the curry for a further 5 minutes, then season to taste.

serve the curry hot with boiled rice, garnished with yellow pepper strips and fried garlic, and topped with a red chilli curl, if liked.

Serves 4
Preparation time: *10 minutes*
Cooking time: *25 minutes*

Beef and Galangal Salad

Sticky (glutinous) rice, which is widely used in the dishes of the north and northeast of Thailand, is a type of short-grain rice that is gluten free.

300 g (10 oz) minced beef

2 tablespoons Ground Roast Rice – use sticky (glutinous) rice (see page 248)

5 thin slices of fresh galangal or root ginger

3 tablespoons finely chopped spring onion

1 teaspoon ground chilli

3–4 tablespoons lemon juice

3 tablespoons nam pla (fish sauce)

½ teaspoon palm sugar or light muscovado sugar

4–5 mint sprigs, leaves chopped, plus extra sprigs to garnish

3 tablespoons chopped shallots

1 crisp lettuce, separated into leaves, to serve

put the minced beef in a saucepan and cook over a low heat for 10–15 minutes, stirring constantly, until the meat is broken up, cooked and all the liquid has been absorbed. Transfer the beef to a bowl, stir in all the remaining ingredients, except the lettuce, and mix well.

arrange a bed of lettuce on a shallow dish and top with the beef mixture. Garnish with mint sprigs and serve immediately.

Serves 4
Preparation time: *10 minutes*
Cooking time: *10–15 minutes*

Chiang Mai Jungle Curry with Beef

2 tablespoons groundnut oil

500 g (1 lb) lean beef, thinly sliced

400 ml (14 fl oz) coconut milk

salt and pepper

Spice paste

2 tablespoons yellow bean sauce

3 tablespoons Red Curry Paste (see page 12)

2 tablespoons palm sugar or light muscovado sugar

4 shallots, chopped

2 garlic cloves, chopped

2 large fresh red chillies, deseeded and chopped

1 lemon grass stalk, chopped, or ¼ teaspoon grated lemon rind

2.5 cm (1 inch) piece of fresh galangal or root ginger, peeled and chopped

½ teaspoon dried shrimp paste

4 tablespoons lime juice

boiled rice, to serve

To garnish

½ red pepper, cored, deseeded and cut into fine strips

2 spring onions, cut into very fine strips

make the spice paste. Put all the paste ingredients in a food processor and process to a thick paste. Alternatively, put them in a mortar and pound with a pestle.

heat the oil in a large, flameproof casserole and stir-fry the beef over a moderate heat for 3 minutes to seal the meat. Add the spice paste and stir-fry for a further 3 minutes.

pour the coconut milk into the casserole, stir to mix and bring to the boil. Reduce the heat, cover and simmer the curry gently, stirring occasionally, for 50 minutes, or until the beef is tender. Season to taste.

serve the curry hot with boiled rice, garnished with fine strips of red pepper and very fine strips of spring onion.

Serves 3
Preparation time: *15 minutes*
Cooking time: *about 1 hour*

Beef and Bamboo Shoot Salad

Bamboo shoots are readily available in cans, when they are peeled and partially cooked. You can also sometimes find fresh or vacuum-packed shoots in large stores.

200 g (7 oz) fillet or rump steak, thinly sliced

200 ml (7 fl oz) coconut milk

250 g (8 oz) can bamboo shoots, drained and sliced

1½ tablespoons Red Curry Paste (see page 12)

2 tablespoons chopped lemon grass

1½ teaspoons finely grated lemon rind

2 tablespoons lemon juice

1½ teaspoons nam pla (fish sauce)

3 small fresh red bird's eye chillies, finely sliced into rings

1 lettuce, separated into leaves, to serve

To garnish

shredded spring onion

finely sliced kaffir lime leaves (optional)

put the steak in a small saucepan with the coconut milk and cook over a low heat for 10–15 minutes, or until the steak is tender and has absorbed most of the coconut milk. (Any liquid remaining in the pan should have an oily appearance.) Remove the pan from the heat and leave to cool.

transfer the meat to a bowl. Add all the remaining ingredients, except the chilli and lettuce, and mix well.

arrange a bed of lettuce on a shallow serving dish, top with the beef mixture and scatter over the chilli. Garnish with shredded spring onion and finely sliced lime leaves, if liked. Serve immediately.

Serves 4
Preparation time: *15 minutes*
Cooking time: *10–15 minutes*

Hot Thai Beef Salad

2 tablespoons vegetable oil

500 g (1 lb) rump or fillet steak, cut across the grain into thin strips

2 garlic cloves, finely chopped

2 fresh green chillies, finely sliced into rings

juice of 2 lemons

1 tablespoon nam pla (fish sauce)

2 teaspoons caster sugar

2 ripe papayas, peeled, deseeded and finely sliced

½ large cucumber, cut into matchsticks

75 g (3 oz) fresh bean sprouts

1 crisp lettuce, shredded

Chilli sauce

8 fresh red chillies, chopped

4 garlic cloves, crushed

1 tablespoon nam pla (fish sauce)

2 teaspoons palm sugar or light muscovado sugar

2 tablespoons lime or lemon juice

¼ teaspoon salt

125 ml (4 fl oz) water

2 tablespoons groundnut oil

make the sauce. Put the chillies, garlic, nam pla, sugar, lime or lemon juice and salt in a small saucepan. Stir in the measurement water and oil. Bring to the boil, then reduce the heat and simmer for 10–15 minutes. Transfer to a food processor or blender and process until smooth. Transfer to a serving bowl.

heat the oil in a wok or large frying pan and stir-fry the steak, garlic and chillies over a high heat for 3–4 minutes, or until the steak is browned on all sides.

pour in the lemon juice and nam pla, add the sugar and stir-fry for 1–2 minutes.

remove the pan from the heat. Lift the steak out of the liquid with a slotted spoon and toss with the papayas, cucumber, bean sprouts and lettuce in a large serving bowl. Drizzle the liquid from the pan over the salad ingredients as a dressing and serve hot with the chilli sauce.

Serves 4
Preparation time: *10 minutes*
Cooking time: *about 20 minutes*

Chicken and Duck

Phuket Chicken and Lemon Grass Curry

3 tablespoons vegetable oil

4 garlic cloves, crushed

3 shallots, chopped

3 lemon grass stalks, finely chopped, or ¾ teaspoon grated lemon rind

6 kaffir lime leaves, shredded, or ¼ teaspoon grated lime rind

3 tablespoons Green Curry Paste (see page 13)

1 tablespoon nam pla (fish sauce)

2 teaspoons palm sugar or light muscovado sugar

250 ml (8 fl oz) Chicken Stock (see page 14)

8 large chicken drumsticks

salt and pepper (optional)

noodles, to serve

To garnish

1 fresh red chilli, diagonally sliced

kaffir lime leaves (optional)

lemon grass stalks, tied in a knot (optional)

heat the oil in a wok or large frying pan and stir-fry the garlic and shallots over a low heat for 3 minutes, or until softened.

add the lemon grass or lemon rind, lime leaves or lime rind, curry paste, nam pla and sugar to the pan and stir-fry for 1 minute, then add the stock and chicken drumsticks and bring the curry to the boil. Reduce the heat, cover and simmer gently, stirring occasionally, for 40–45 minutes until the chicken is tender and cooked through.

taste and adjust the seasoning, if necessary. Serve the curry hot with noodles, garnished with the sliced red chilli, and lime leaves and knotted lemon grass stalks, if liked.

Serves 4
Preparation time: *15 minutes*
Cooking time: *about 1 hour*

Minced Chicken with Basil

5 small fresh green chillies

2 garlic cloves

2 tablespoons vegetable oil

125 g (4 oz) minced chicken

1 shallot, chopped

25 g (1 oz) bamboo shoots

25 g (1 oz) red pepper, cored, deseeded and chopped

15 g (½ oz) carrot, diced

1 teaspoon palm sugar or light muscovado sugar

3 tablespoons nam pla (fish sauce)

3 tablespoons Chicken Stock (see page 14)

15 g (½ oz) basil leaves, finely chopped

boiled rice, to serve

To garnish

Crispy Garlic (see page 250)

Crispy Shallots (see page 250)

Crispy Basil (see page 248)

put the chillies and garlic into a mortar and pound together with a pestle until well broken down.

heat the oil in a wok or large frying pan and stir-fry the chillies and garlic over a moderate heat for 30 seconds. Add all the remaining ingredients and stir-fry for 4 minutes. Increase the heat to high and stir-fry for a further 30 seconds.

turn the stir-fry on to a serving dish and serve with boiled rice, garnished with crispy garlic, crispy shallots and crispy basil.

Serves 4
Preparation time: *10 minutes*
Cooking time: *6 minutes*

clipboard: Thai cooks usually flavour their oil with garlic and shallots before using it. The crispy garlic and shallots are removed from the oil, reserved and then sprinkled over many different dishes. If you like, you can deep-fry just garlic or just shallots, or you can deep-fry them both, then store them together rather than separately.

Stir-fried Chicken with Cashew Nuts and Baby Corn

This Chinese-influenced dish looks impressive but is easy to prepare.

3 tablespoons vegetable oil

125 g (4 oz) boneless chicken, skinned and cut into bite-sized pieces

¼ onion, sliced

50 g (2 oz) baby corn cobs, diagonally sliced

50 g (2 oz) cashew nuts

125 ml (4 fl oz) soy sauce

4 tablespoons Chicken Stock (see page 14)

4 teaspoons palm sugar or light muscovado sugar

15 g (½ oz) spring onion, diagonally sliced

pepper

1 large fresh red chilli, diagonally sliced, to garnish

heat the oil in a wok or large frying pan and stir-fry the chicken, onion, baby corn and cashew nuts over a high heat for 3 minutes.

reduce the heat and stir in the soy sauce. Then add the stock, sugar and spring onion and season with pepper. Increase the heat and stir-fry for a further 2 minutes.

turn the stir-fry on to a serving dish, sprinkle with the sliced red chilli and serve immediately.

Serves 4
Preparation time: *10 minutes*
Cooking time: *5–6 minutes*

Thai Touches

Nam pla

One of the most important elements in Thai cooking is the fish sauce that is called nam pla in Thailand. The Vietnamese equivalent, nuoc naam, is almost identical and can be used in all recipes that require nam pla. The sauce is pungent and salty and often replaces most or all of the salt that a Western cook would automatically add to a dish.

As well as being included in recipes, however, nam pla can be offered, straight from the bottle, as a dipping sauce in a small bowl, garnished with two or three finely chopped small chillies and a dash of lime juice.

Chilli sauce

After nam pla, chilli sauce is the most popular of all dipping sauces. A basic recipe is given on page 138, but it is possible to buy ready-made sauces that vary in strength and intensity. If you make your own, aim to balance the spicy, salty and sour flavours of the ingredients. Offer neatly chopped raw vegetables, such as cucumbers, cabbage and green beans, pieces of cooked aubergine or sweet potato, slices of omelette, portions of grilled fish or meat and even fruit to dip into a dish of your own sauce.

Using chillies

Chillies are included in many of the recipes in this book and are used in amounts that will give an authentic Thai flavour. They are also used as garnishes in many of the recipes, when they are deseeded and finely sliced, sometimes on the diagonal for added interest, or used whole, which the unwary should avoid eating as part of the dish. Fine strips of red or green chilli can be put into iced water and left for them to curl up, to make an eye-catching garnish.

Green chillies are hotter than the riper red chillies, although this may be something of an illusion, created by the fact that a chilli as it ripens becomes sweeter and more rounded in flavour, so the heat is less obvious. Quantities can always be adjusted to suit your personal preferences.

Of the red chillies, smaller chillies tend to be hotter than the larger, more elongated ones. The rounded Scotch bonnet and pointed bird's eye (mouse dropping) chillies pack powerful punches for their size. Among chillies usually available in supermarkets, the Fresno, which ranges in colour from glossy green to orange and red, is medium-hot and the jalapeño, though slightly smaller, is another hot one.

Dried chillies are hotter than fresh ones. Just one or two whole small dried red chillies or a small quantity of crushed dried chillies, dried chilli flakes or ground chilli will add a lot of heat to a recipe.

Scraping the seeds from a chilli, as well as removing the white membrane, will reduce its heat, because these are the hottest parts of a chilli.

Finally, always handle chillies with care. Wear disposable gloves if your hands are sensitive, and be careful not to touch any part of your face, particularly your eyes, before you have washed your hands.

Using banana leaves as a serving dish adds an authentic touch to cooking Thai food at home. Buy them at large oriental supermarkets.

Using banana leaves

Banana leaves are widely used in Thai cuisine as a way of both cooking and serving food. In addition to adding a touch of the exotic to a meal, the leaf imparts a subtle flavour to the dish, either acting in the same way as a piece of foil when wrapped around a filling and cooked, or used as a serving dish or container, having been cut and shaped (see pages 168 and 234). Whole leaves can be bought, rolled, in packs of four or five from large oriental stores and should be warmed over a flame or electric hob before they are used to lighten the colour and soften them. Alternatively, the leaves can be dipped in boiling water, then patted dry with kitchen paper.

Pandanus leaves, which have a flowery flavour and a strong green colour, can be used in the same way as banana leaves.

Creative garnishes

Slivers of fresh coconut, which can also be toasted, or grated fresh coconut make attractive decorations for both sweet and savoury Thai dishes (see pages 188 and 238), and wafer-thin ribbons of mooli or cucumber, which can be easily made with a swivel-bladed vegetable peeler, are also effective garnishes (see pages 46 and 176). Flowering chives are another interesting decorative item, and can be used for tying around little wonton pouches (see page 44), while a few lemon grass stalks are sometimes tied together in a knot to provide a finishing touch (see page 142).

Chillies, introduced by the Portuguese in the 16th century are used in very large quantities in Thai cooking.

Coconut Grilled Chicken

The stems and roots of coriander are used together with the leaves to add a pungent flavour to Thai dishes. The dried seeds are also often used, but are never substituted for the fresh herb.

2–3 boneless chicken breasts

Marinade

400 ml (14 fl oz) coconut milk

4 garlic cloves, finely chopped

4 small fresh green or red chillies, finely chopped

2.5 cm (1 inch) piece of fresh root ginger, peeled and sliced

grated rind and juice of 1 lime

2 tablespoons palm sugar or light muscovado sugar

3 tablespoons soy sauce

1 tablespoon nam pla (fish sauce)

25 g (1 oz) fresh coriander leaves, stalks and roots

Chicken Stock (see page 14), for thinning (optional)

To garnish

1 fresh red chilli, deseeded and finely diced

very fine strips of spring onion

make the marinade. Mix all the marinade ingredients together in a bowl.

make 3 diagonal cuts in each side of the chicken breasts, put them in a dish and pour over the marinade. Cover and leave to marinate in the refrigerator for 2 hours.

arrange the chicken pieces in a foil-lined grill pan, making sure that they are thickly spread with the marinade, and cook under a preheated hot grill, turning occasionally, for about 15 minutes, or until cooked through. The skin side will take a little longer to cook than the other side.

meanwhile, put the remaining marinade in a small saucepan, bring to the boil, stirring constantly, adding a little stock if it is too thick, and continue to boil for 2–3 minutes. The sauce must brought to a high temperature to cook any raw chicken juices.

when the chicken is cooked, cut it into slices and arrange the pieces on a serving dish. Serve the chicken garnished with very fine strips of spring onion and diced red chilli, with the sauce in a separate bowl.

Serves 4
Preparation time: *10 minutes, plus marinating*
Cooking time: *15 minutes*

Barbecued Chicken

1.5 kg (3 lb) whole chicken, spatchcocked, or part-boned chicken breasts

5 cm (2 inch) piece of fresh galangal, peeled and finely chopped

4 garlic cloves, crushed

1 large fresh red chilli, finely chopped

4 shallots, finely chopped

2 tablespoons finely chopped fresh coriander leaves

150 ml (¼ pint) thick coconut milk (see page 16)

salt and pepper

flowering chives, to garnish

To serve

Chilli Sauce (see page 138)

boiled sticky (glutinous) rice

lime wedges

rub the chicken all over with salt and pepper and put it in a shallow dish.

put the galangal, garlic, chilli, shallots and coriander in a food processor and process to a paste. Add the coconut milk and mix until well blended. Pour the marinade over the chicken, cover and leave to marinate in the refrigerator overnight.

remove the chicken from the marinade and cook on a hot barbecue for 30–40 minutes for spatchcocked chicken, or until the juices run clear when a skewer is inserted into one of the legs, and 10–15 minutes for chicken breasts, turning and basting them regularly with the marinade.

leave the chicken to rest for 5 minutes, then chop it into small pieces with a cleaver. Serve with the chilli sauce, sticky rice and lime wedges. Garnish with flowering chives and eat with your fingers.

Serves 3–4
Preparation time: *15 minutes, plus marinating*
Cooking time: *30–40 minutes for spatchcocked chicken;*
10–15 minutes for chicken breasts

Red Curry Duck

This rich dish is very popular in Thailand. It gets its colour and flavour from the red curry paste, making it one of the milder curries.

¼ roast duck

1 tablespoon vegetable oil

1½ tablespoons Red Curry Paste (see page 12)

150 ml (¼ pint) coconut milk

1 tablespoon palm sugar or light muscovado sugar

3 kaffir lime leaves, torn, or ¼ teaspoon grated lime rind

65 g (2½ oz) peas, fresh or frozen

1 large fresh red chilli, diagonally sliced

4 tablespoons Chicken Stock (see page 14)

2 tomatoes, finely diced

125 g (4 oz) fresh or canned pineapple, cut into chunks, plus extra to serve

1 tablespoon nam pla (fish sauce)

noodles, to serve

To garnish

fine strips of red pepper

very fine strips of spring onion

remove the skin and meat from the duck, chop them into bite-sized pieces and set both the skin and meat aside.

heat the oil in a wok or large frying pan and stir-fry the curry paste over a moderate heat for 30 seconds. Add 3 tablespoons of the coconut milk, mix it with the paste, then add the remainder and cook, stirring, over a low heat for 1 minute.

add the duck skin and meat and cook, stirring, for 2 minutes. Add the sugar, lime leaves or lime rind, peas, chilli, stock, tomatoes and pineapple. Mix well, then add the nam pla. Stir thoroughly to combine, then transfer to a serving bowl.

serve with extra pineapple and noodles, garnished with fine strips of red pepper and very fine strips of spring onion.

Serves 3–4
Preparation time: *15 minutes*
Cooking time: *5 minutes*

Fish and Shellfish

Stir-fried Squid with Basil

Take care to cook the squid over a high heat and only briefly, as it can easily turn rubbery in texture if overcooked.

2 tablespoons oil

6 garlic cloves, chopped

12 small fresh green chillies, finely sliced

1–2 shallots, chopped

125 g (4 oz) squid, cleaned and cut into strips

½ green pepper, cored, deseeded and chopped

2 tablespoons Fish Stock (see page 15)

1 tablespoon nam pla (fish sauce)

1 tablespoon palm sugar or light muscovado sugar

15 g (½ oz) basil leaves

1 tablespoon Crispy Shallots (see page 250),
to garnish

heat the oil in a wok or large frying pan and stir-fry the garlic, chillies and shallots over a moderate heat for 30 seconds.

add the squid and green pepper, increase the heat to high and stir-fry for 1 minute, then reduce the heat and add the stock, nam pla and basil. Cook, stirring, for 1 minute.

serve immediately, garnished with the crispy shallots.

Serves 2
Preparation time: *8 minutes*
Cooking time: *3–4 minutes*

Grilled Fish in Ginger and Oyster Sauce

1 whole grey mullet, cleaned

½ tablespoon Garlic Mixture (see page 250)

½ onion, chopped

5 mushrooms, sliced

2 tablespoons finely sliced fresh root ginger

1 celery stick, sliced

1 teaspoon pepper

1 tablespoon soy sauce

1 tablespoon oyster sauce

250 ml (8 fl oz) Fish Stock (see page 15)

lemon slices, to garnish

score the skin of the mullet with a sharp knife to allow the sauce to be absorbed during cooking. Rub the fish with the garlic mixture, pressing it well into the cuts. Transfer the fish to a shallow heatproof dish.

mix the remaining ingredients together in a bowl and pour the mixture over the fish. Cook under a preheated moderate grill for 20 minutes, turning the fish over halfway through the cooking time.

carefully transfer the fish to a warm serving dish, pour over the sauce, garnish with lemon slices and serve immediately.

Serves 2
Preparation time: *20 minutes*
Cooking time: *20 minutes*

clipboard: Snapper can be used instead in this recipe if you cannot find mullet.

Fish with Tamarind Water and Ginger

2 whole grey mullet or mackerel, cleaned

4 shallots, chopped

1 tablespoon dried shrimp paste

1 teaspoon pepper

750 ml (1¼ pints) water

2 tablespoons finely chopped fresh root ginger

2 tablespoons tamarind water (see page 32)

4 tablespoons nam pla (fish sauce)

3 tablespoons palm sugar or light muscovado sugar

4 spring onions, chopped, plus extra to garnish

To serve

boiled rice

pickled chillies (optional)

remove the head and tail from each mullet or mackerel and cut the fish lengthways in half. Score the skin with a sharp knife to allow the sauce to be absorbed during cooking.

put the shallots, shrimp paste and pepper in a food processor and process to a paste. Alternatively, pound in a mortar with a pestle. Stir the paste into the measurement water in a saucepan large enough to hold the pieces of fish and bring it to the boil.

add the fish, ginger, tamarind water, nam pla, sugar and spring onions. Reduce the heat and simmer for about 20 minutes.

serve the fish hot with boiled rice and pickled chillies, if liked, and garnished with chopped spring onions.

Serves 4
Preparation time: *20 minutes*
Cooking time: *25 minutes*

Steamed Pomfret with Lemon Grass

Sometimes known as Ray's bream, pomfret is a deep-bodied but thin fish, popular for its firm, white flesh, which comes easily away from the bones. Use any flat fish instead if necessary.

375 g (12 oz) whole pomfret, cleaned

1 teaspoon salt

1 lemon grass stalk, cut into 3 pieces

15 small fresh red and green chillies

1 fresh coriander root, crushed and chopped

3 garlic cloves, finely sliced

3 tablespoons nam pla (fish sauce)

2 tablespoons soy sauce

ground chilli, to serve

cut diagonal slashes into each side of the fish and rub the salt all over to firm it up. Leave for 2 minutes, then wash off the salt.

put the fish on a plate, arrange the lemon grass on top, then put it into a steamer. Steam for 35–40 minutes.

meanwhile, chop the chillies very finely and put them into a small bowl with the coriander, garlic, nam pla and soy sauce. Stir thoroughly.

pour the sauce over the fish and serve with the ground chilli on the side.

Serves 3–4
Preparation time: *5 minutes*
Cooking time: *35–40 minutes*

clipboard: Supermarkets generally sell lemon grass in packs of of 4–6 stalks. Before use, the straw-like tops need to be trimmed as well as the ends, and sometimes the outside leaves are very woody and need to be removed. Dried and ground lemon grass is also available, or you can use lemon rind or juice instead.

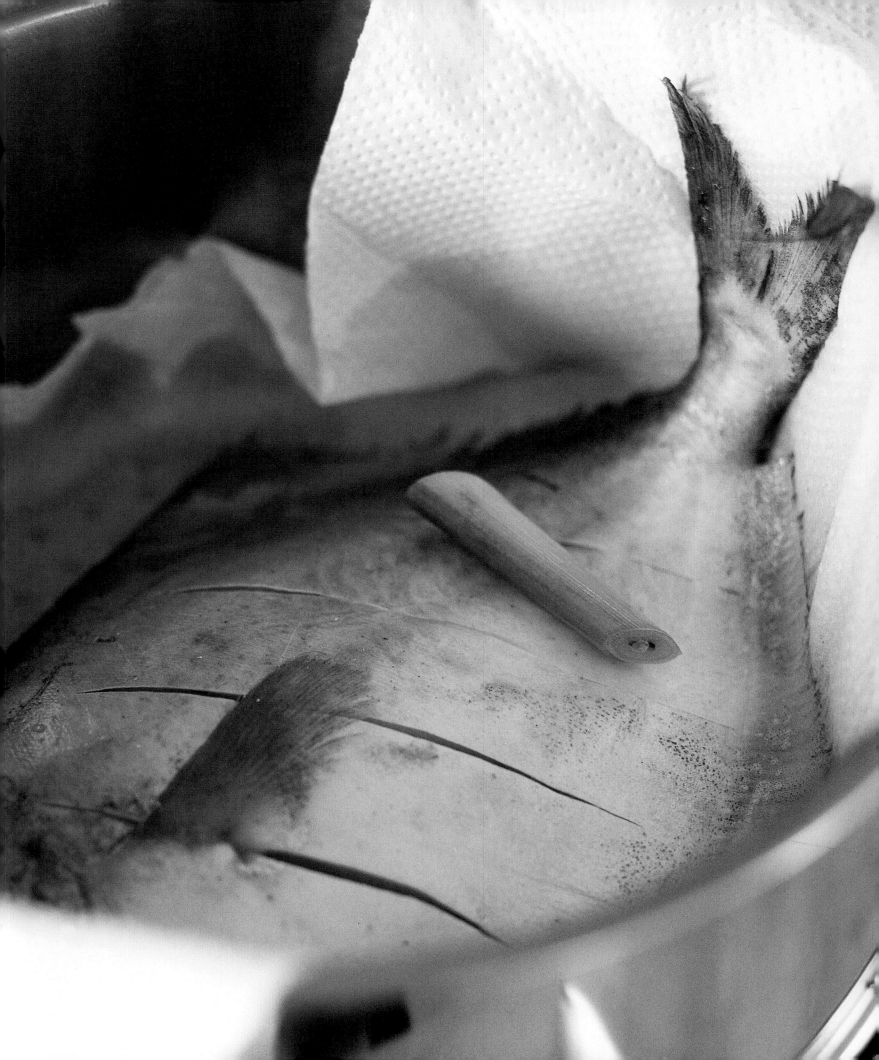

Fish in Garlic Sauce

John Dory is a deep-bodied delicate fish and has a slightly sweet falvour. It makes a good alternative to mullet or lemon sole in this fragrant dish.

1 whole mullet, lemon sole or John Dory, cleaned

vegetable oil, for deep-frying, plus 3 tablespoons

2 tablespoons Garlic Mixture (see page 250)

2 tablespoons nam pla (fish sauce)

1 teaspoon palm sugar or light muscovado sugar

2 celery sticks, thinly sliced

To garnish

fresh coriander sprigs

1 fresh red chilli, cut into fine strips.

neatly score the skin of the fish diagonally in both directions to allow the sauce to be absorbed during cooking. Pat dry with kitchen paper.

heat the oil for deep-frying in a wok or large frying pan to 180–190°C (350–375°F), or until a cube of bread browns in 30 seconds. Deep-fry the fish for 10–15 minutes until golden brown, turning halfway through the cooking time. Remove with a slotted spoon and drain on kitchen paper.

meanwhile, heat the 3 tablespoons oil in a saucepan large enough to hold the whole fish. Stir in the garlic mixture and cook, stirring, until it changes colour. Stir in the nam pla and sugar. Add the fish to the pan, turning until well coated in the mixture.

transfer the fish to a serving dish and keep warm. Add the celery to the sauce remaining in the pan and stir-fry for 2 minutes, then pour the mixture over the fish. Garnish with coriander sprigs and fine strips of red chilli. Serve warm.

Serves 4
Preparation time: *15 minutes*
Cooking time: *20 minutes*

Spicy Fishcakes

If you prefer, you can replace half the cod fillet with 250 g (8 oz) raw king prawns, peeled and deveined, to make spicy prawn cakes instead.

500 g (I lb) cod fillet, skinned and cut into chunks

3 tablespoons Red Curry Paste (see page 12)

I egg

3 tablespoons nam pla (fish sauce)

1–2 tablespoons rice flour

75 g (3 oz) thin green beans, finely chopped

I tablespoon finely shredded kaffir lime leaves or ¼ teaspoon grated lime rind

oil, for deep-frying

To serve

Chilli Sauce (see page 138)

lime slices

cucumber salad (optional)

put the cod and curry paste in a food processor and process to a thick paste. Alternatively, put in a mortar and pound with a pestle.

transfer the fish mixture to a bowl and add the egg, nam pla and enough of the flour to knead with your hands into a stiff mixture. Work in the green beans and lime leaves or lime rind.

form the fish mixture into 16–20 balls and, using your hands, flatten each ball into a round about 1 cm (½ inch) thick.

heat the oil in a wok or deep frying pan to 180–190°C (350–375°F), or until a cube of bread browns in 30 seconds. Deep-fry the fishcakes, a few at a time, for 4–5 minutes on each side until cooked and golden brown. Take care not to overcook them. Remove the fishcakes with a slotted spoon and drain on kitchen paper. Serve hot with the chilli sauce, lime slices and a cucumber salad, if liked.

Serves 4–5
Preparation time: *20 minutes*
Cooking time: *16–20 minutes*

Crab Curry

If you cannot find crab claws, use 500 g (1 lb) raw peeled and deveined king prawns instead.

1 tablespoon vegetable oil

1½ teaspoons Red Curry Paste (see page 12)

6 tablespoons coconut milk

1 kaffir lime leaf, torn

12 raw crab claws

150 ml (¼ pint) Fish Stock (see page 15)

2 tablespoons palm sugar or light muscovado sugar

1 teaspoon salt

65 g (2½ oz) bamboo shoots

To garnish

½ large fresh red chilli, diagonally sliced

fresh coriander leaves

heat the oil in a wok or large frying pan and stir-fry the curry paste over a moderately high heat for 30 seconds. Add all the remaining ingredients, stir well and simmer for 10 minutes. If the liquid level reduces significantly, add more stock.

turn the mixture into a serving bowl and serve, garnished with the sliced red chilli and coriander leaves.

Serves 3–4
Preparation time: *3 minutes*
Cooking time: *12 minutes*

clipboard: Kaffir lime leaves add a fragrant citrus flavour to Thai dishes. They are available dried from large supermarkets, but can be bought fresh in oriental food stores. If they are unavailable, use lime rind or juice.

Fresh Crab Curry with Chillies

For added impact, you can serve the curry in the crab shell from the fresh crab. Wash the crab shell and dry thoroughly with kitchen paper before using.

1 teaspoon curry powder

250 ml (8 fl oz) water

500 g (1 lb) raw crab meat (see below)

4 spring onions, chopped

2 fresh red chillies, deseeded and finely sliced

1½ teaspoons palm sugar or light muscovado sugar

1 tablespoon white wine

½ teaspoon salt

¼ teaspoon pepper

1 egg

1 tablespoon single cream

To garnish

dried mango slices

prawn crackers

fresh red chillies, sliced into rings

mix the curry powder with the measurement water in a saucepan and bring to the boil. Stir in the crab meat.

return to the boil and add the spring onions, chillies, sugar, wine, salt and pepper. Reduce the heat and simmer for 10 minutes.

meanwhile, mix the egg and cream together in a small bowl. Beat in 2 tablespoons of the curry sauce and return the mixture to the saucepan. Cook, stirring, over a low heat for 1 minute.

transfer the crab to a serving bowl and garnish with dried mango slices, prawn crackers and sliced red chillies.

Serves 4
Preparation time: *15 minutes*
Cooking time: *15–20 minutes*

clipboard: To prepare the crab meat, remove the legs and claws from the crab. Remove the undershell and discard the gills. Clean the body and cut the meat into small chunks. Crack the legs and claws and extract the meat.

Prawn Vermicelli

Although it seems fiddly, using pork belly fat instead of vegetable oil imparts a highly distinctive flavour to this dish.

50 g (2 oz) pork belly fat

8 tablespoons milk

1 teaspoon dark soy sauce

3 tablespoons oyster sauce

1 teaspoon chopped garlic

5 black peppercorns, crushed

15 g (½ oz) fresh coriander leaves, stalks and roots, plus extra leaves to garnish

20 g (¾ oz) fresh root ginger, peeled and cut into fine matchsticks

125 g (4 oz) dried glass noodles, soaked in hot water for about 15 minutes and drained

12 raw prawns, peeled, but tails left intact

2 tablespoons Fish Stock (see page 15 – optional)

heat the fat in a wok or large frying pan over a moderate heat until the oil runs, stirring occasionally. Remove the wok from the heat and set aside. Discard the fat, but leave the oil in the wok to cool for about 5 minutes.

meanwhile, combine the milk, soy sauce and oyster sauce in a bowl.

when the oil has cooled, add the garlic, crushed peppercorns, coriander and ginger and stir-fry for 30 seconds. Add the noodles and milk mixture, stir together thoroughly over a high heat, then reduce the heat to low, cover and cook for 12 minutes.

increase the heat, add the prawns, and the stock if the sauce looks too thick, and cook, stirring, for about 2–3 minutes until the prawns have turned pink and are cooked through.

turn the mixture into a serving bowl and serve immediately, garnished with coriander leaves.

Serves 4
Preparation time: *10 minutes*
Cooking time: *20 minutes*

Thai Red Prawn and Cucumber Curry

2 tablespoons groundnut oil

1 shallot, chopped

2 garlic cloves, chopped

2 tablespoons Red Curry Paste (see page 12)

1 fresh red chilli, deseeded and chopped

3 kaffir lime leaves, finely shredded, or ¼ teaspoon grated lime rind

300 ml (½ pint) coconut milk

20 raw king prawns, peeled and deveined

125 g (4 oz) cucumber, halved lengthways, deseeded and thickly sliced

1 tablespoon nam pla (fish sauce)

1 teaspoon palm sugar or light muscovado sugar

noodles, to serve

To garnish (optional)

shredded kaffir lime leaves

cucumber ribbons

heat the oil in a wok or large frying pan and stir-fry the shallot and garlic over a low heat for about 3 minutes until softened. Add the curry paste, chilli and lime leaves or lime rind and stir-fry for a further minute.

add the coconut milk, increase the heat and bring the sauce to the boil, then reduce the heat and simmer the sauce gently, stirring occasionally, for 5 minutes.

add the prawns, cucumber, nam pla and sugar to the pan. Stir to coat the ingredients evenly in the sauce, then simmer the curry gently for 5 minutes, or until the prawns have turned pink and are cooked through and the cucumber is tender. Taste and adjust the seasoning, if necessary.

serve the curry hot with noodles, garnished with shredded lime leaves and cucumber ribbons, if liked.

Serves 4
Preparation time: *10 minutes*
Cooking time: *15 minutes*

Prawns in Coconut Sauce

Although nam pla has an extremely pungent flavour,

its distinctive taste is characteristic of many traditional

Thai dishes, including seafood ones.

16 raw large prawns

2 tablespoons vegetable oil

1 large onion, finely chopped

2 lemon grass stalks, chopped, plus extra whole stalks to garnish (optional)

2 fresh red chillies, sliced

2.5 cm (1 inch) piece of fresh root ginger, peeled and shredded

1 tablespoon ground cumin

1 tablespoon ground coriander

2 tablespoons nam pla (fish sauce)

250 ml (8 fl oz) thick coconut milk (see page 16)

3 tablespoons Crushed Roasted Nuts (see page 248)

2 tomatoes, skinned and chopped

1 teaspoon palm sugar or light muscovado sugar

To serve

1 tablespoon lime juice

fresh coriander leaves, chopped

peel the prawns, leaving the tails intact. Remove the dark vein running along the back.

heat the oil in a wok or large frying pan and stir-fry the onion over a moderate heat for 1 minute, or until soft and golden. Add the chopped lemon grass, chillies, ginger, cumin and ground coriander and stir-fry for 2 minutes.

add the nam pla and coconut milk to the pan. Stir well and then add the nuts and tomatoes. Cook, stirring occasionally, over a low heat until the tomatoes are soft and the flavours of the sauce are well developed.

stir in the prawns and simmer gently for 5 minutes, or until they have turned pink and are cooked through. Add the sugar and transfer to a warm serving dish.

serve hot, sprinkled with lime juice and chopped coriander, and garnished with lemon grass stalks, if liked.

Serves 4
Preparation time: *20 minutes*
Cooking time: *20 minutes*

Spicy Prawn Curry

750 ml (1¼ pints) coconut milk

2 tablespoons Green Curry Paste (see page 13)

2 teaspoons ground galangal

750 g (1½ lb) raw large prawns

2 tablespoons nam pla (fish sauce)

boiled rice, to serve (optional)

To garnish
kaffir lime leaves

4 basil leaves, shredded

put the coconut milk in a jug and chill in the refrigerator for at least 1 hour, or until the thick milk rises to the surface. Scoop 250 ml (8 fl oz) off the top and put it into a wok or heavy-based saucepan. Reserve the remaining coconut milk for later.

bring the coconut milk to the boil, then reduce the heat and simmer, uncovered, stirring occasionally, until the coconut oil begins to bubble to the surface and the liquid reduces to a quarter of its original volume. Stir in the curry paste and galangal and bring to the boil. Cook over a moderate to high heat until most of the liquid evaporates.

peel the prawns and remove the dark vein running along the back. Rinse under cold running water, pat dry on kitchen paper and add to the mixture in the pan. Stir-fry for 3–4 minutes until the prawns have turned pink and are cooked through.

stir in the remaining coconut milk and the nam pla and simmer for 6–8 minutes, stirring occasionally.

serve garnished with lime leaves and shredded basil leaves, accompanied by boiled rice, if liked.

Serves 4–6
Preparation time: *10 minutes, plus chilling*
Cooking time: *30–35 minutes*

Braised Chive Flowers with Prawns

1 tablespoon groundnut oil

2 garlic cloves, crushed

175 g (6 oz) flowering chives, large chives or spring onions, cut into 7 cm (3 inch) lengths

1 tablespoon nam pla (fish sauce)

3 tablespoons dark soy sauce

2 tablespoons caster sugar

250 g (8 oz) raw small prawns, peeled and roughly chopped

1 fresh red chilli, sliced, to garnish

boiled jasmine (fragrant) rice, to serve

heat the oil in a wok or large frying pan and stir-fry the garlic over a moderate heat for 1 minute. Add the chives or spring onions, nam pla, soy sauce and sugar and stir-fry for a further minute.

add the prawns to the pan and stir-fry for 3 minutes until they have turned pink and are cooked through. Serve immediately, garnished with sliced red chilli and accompanied by boiled jasmine rice.

Serves 3–4
Preparation time: *10 minutes*
Cooking time: *5 minutes*

clipboard: Thai jasmine rice, sometimes known as fragrant rice, is more expensive than other types of long-grain rice, but it is so delicious that it is well worth paying extra for it. If you cook a lot of oriental food, you might even consider buying a 5 kg (11 lb) or 10 kg (22 lb) sack from an oriental food store, because this is the most economical way of buying it and it will keep for a year or more.

Mussels with Thai Herbs

The fresh, aromatic herbs combine perfectly with the meaty flesh of the mussels in this dish. Serve with jasmine (fragrant) rice or plain boiled rice to soak up the juices.

2 kg (4 lb) live mussels

1.2 litres (2 pints) water

6 kaffir lime leaves or ½ teaspoon grated lime rind

rind of 1 lemon

2 lemon grass stalks

1 tablespoon salt

3 fresh red chillies, sliced

3 spring onions, chopped

fresh coriander leaves, to garnish

boiled rice, to serve

wash the mussels in cold water and scrape away any barnacles with a sharp knife. Remove the beards, then leave the mussels to soak in cold water for about 1 hour. Drain and tap any open shells to make sure that they close. Discard any mussels that remain open.

pour the measurement water into a large saucepan and bring to the boil. Add the lime leaves or lime rind, lemon rind, lemon grass and salt. Then add the mussels, cover and return to the boil.

cook the mussels, shaking the pan occasionally, until they have opened. Drain, reserving half the cooking liquid. Transfer the mussels to a deep serving dish, discarding any that remain closed.

strain the reserved stock, discarding the lime leaves or lime rind, lemon rind and lemon grass. Bring to the boil, add the chillies and spring onions and boil vigorously for 2 minutes. Pour over the mussels. Serve immediately, garnished with coriander and accompanied by boiled rice.

Serves 4
Preparation time: *20 minutes, plus soaking*
Cooking time: *20 minutes*

Rice and
Noodles

Coconut Rice

Basmati rice actually comes from India, but it is the ideal accompaniment for most Thai dishes if jasmine (fragrant) rice is not available.

450 ml (¾ pint) coconut milk

½ teaspoon ground turmeric

375 g (12 oz) basmati rice, washed and drained

8 small onions, roughly chopped

20 black peppercorns

1 teaspoon salt

To garnish

fine strips of spring onion

slivers of toasted fresh coconut (optional)

put the coconut milk in a saucepan, stir in the turmeric, then add the rice. Bring to the boil, then reduce the heat, cover and simmer gently for about 10 minutes.

add the onions, peppercorns and salt to the pan and simmer gently for a further 10 minutes, or until the rice is tender. Be careful not to allow the rice to burn.

transfer to a warm serving dish and garnish with fine strips of spring onion and slivers of toasted fresh coconut, if liked.

Serves 4
Preparation time: *10 minutes*
Cooking time: *25 minutes*

Spicy Fried Rice

The weight of 750 g (1½ lb) of boiled rice needed in this recipe is based on a raw weight of about 175 g (6 oz).

125 g (4 oz) minced beef

250 g (8 oz) can red kidney beans, drained

1½ tablespoons nam pla (fish sauce), or to taste

1 tablespoon dark soy sauce

4 fresh red chillies, deseeded and finely chopped

3 garlic cloves, crushed

½ teaspoon salt

2 tablespoons vegetable oil

10 green beans, trimmed and cut into 1 cm (½ inch) lengths

750 g (1½ lb) cold boiled rice

1 tablespoon palm sugar or light muscovado sugar

4 tablespoons roughly chopped basil

salt and pepper (optional)

finely chopped red pepper, to garnish

put the minced beef and kidney beans in a bowl. Mix well and then stir in the nam pla and soy sauce. Cover and leave to stand for 30 minutes to allow the different flavours to blend.

mix the chillies, garlic and salt together in a separate bowl. Heat the oil in a wok or large frying pan and stir-fry the chilli mixture over a moderately high heat for 1 minute.

add the beef and kidney bean mixture to the pan and stir-fry for 3 minutes, or until the beef is lightly browned. Add the green beans and stir-fry over a moderate heat for a further 3 minutes.

add the rice and sugar and stir-fry until the rice is hot and all the ingredients are thoroughly mixed. Add salt and pepper or more nam pla to taste, if necessary. Mix in the basil and transfer to a serving dish. Garnish with chopped red pepper.

Serves 4
Preparation time: *10 minutes, plus marinating*
Cooking time: *10 minutes*

Curried Rice with Black Fungus

Black fungus are a type of dried mushroom, also known as wood fungus, mouse ear and cloud ear. They are used in soups and stir-fries as well as in chicken and fish dishes.

125 g (4 oz) dried black fungus

2 tablespoons groundnut oil

1 onion, chopped

250 g (8 oz) cold boiled rice

1 teaspoon curry powder

1/2 teaspoon soy sauce

2 tomatoes, finely chopped

salt and pepper

1 tablespoon Crispy Garlic (see page 250), to garnish

soak the black fungus in several changes of warm water for 15–20 minutes, then drain and slice.

heat the oil in a wok or large frying pan over a moderate heat, then add all the ingredients, in turn (add the black fungus after the onion), making sure that the rice is well mixed in.

increase the heat to high and stir-fry for 3–4 minutes. Turn into a bowl, garnish with the crispy garlic and serve immediately.

Serves 4
Preparation time: *10 minutes, plus soaking*
Cooking time: *5 minutes*

Yellow Rice with Mushrooms

The spice turmeric, a member of the ginger family, gives this dish its yellow colour. The roots are ground and dried to give the powder that is widely used in all Asian cooking.

2 tablespoons groundnut oil

500 g (1 lb) cold boiled rice

125 g (4 oz) mangetout

125 g (4 oz) button mushrooms, halved

125 g (4 oz) canned, drained bamboo shoots

1 teaspoon ground turmeric

2 teaspoons palm sugar or light muscovado sugar

1 tablespoon soy sauce

1 teaspoon salt

pepper, to taste

To garnish

1 tablespoon Crispy Garlic (see page 250)

1 large fresh red chilli, deseeded and cut into strips

heat the oil in a wok or large frying pan over a moderate heat. Add the rice and stir thoroughly so that it is coated with the oil, then add all the remaining ingredients. Stir-fry over a low heat until thoroughly mixed.

increase the heat and stir-fry for 1–2 minutes, making sure that the rice does not stick to the wok.

turn on to a serving dish, garnish with the crispy garlic and strips of red chilli and serve immediately.

Serves 3–4
Preparation time: *3 minutes*
Cooking time: *5 minutes*

Fried Rice with Beans and Tofu

Tofu is made from crushed soya beans, and although usually sold in soft or silken forms, it is also available ready-fried.

about 750 ml (1¼ pints) groundnut oil, for deep-frying

125 g (4 oz) ready-fried tofu, diced

2 eggs

250 g (8 oz) cold boiled rice

3 teaspoons palm sugar or light muscovado sugar

1½ tablespoons soy sauce

2 teaspoons crushed dried chillies

1 teaspoon vegetarian nam pla (fish sauce) or salt

125 g (4 oz) fine green beans, finely chopped

25 g (1 oz) Crispy Mint (see page 248), to garnish

heat the oil in a wok or deep frying pan to 180–190°C (350–375°F), or until a cube of bread browns in 30 seconds. Deep-fry the tofu until golden brown on all sides. Remove it with a slotted spoon, drain on kitchen paper and set aside.

pour off all but 2 tablespoons of the oil from the pan. Heat the oil until hot, then crack the eggs into it, breaking the yolks and stirring around.

add the rice, sugar, soy sauce, crushed dried chillies and nam pla or salt and increase the heat to high. Stir-fry vigorously for 1 minute.

reduce the heat and add the green beans and tofu. Increase the heat again and stir-fry vigorously for 1 minute. Turn on to a serving dish and serve immediately, garnished with the crispy mint.

Serves 4
Preparation time: *10 minutes*
Cooking time: *about 6 minutes*

Crispy Noodles

Tamarind imparts a slightly sour, tart flavour to foods. If you cannot find the pulp, use tamarind concentrate or lemon juice.

300 ml (½ pint) tamarind water (see page 32)

200 g (7 oz) palm sugar or light muscovado sugar

75 ml (3 fl oz) tomato ketchup

3 tablespoons nam pla (fish sauce)

about 750 ml (1¼ pints) oil, for deep-frying

125 g (4 oz) dried rice vermicelli, soaked in hot water for 15–20 minutes and drained

40 g (1½ oz) ready-fried tofu, cut into 2.5 x 5 mm (1 x ¼ inch) pieces

green shoots of 1 spring onion, sliced, to garnish

heat the tamarind water and sugar in a wok or large frying pan until the sugar dissolves (it will foam up). Add the ketchup and stir for 1 minute, then add the nam pla. Cook, stirring, for 20–25 minutes. The sauce will gradually thicken until it is almost the consistency of jam and will stick to the noodles. Remove the pan from the heat and leave to cool slightly.

heat the oil in a separate wok or large frying pan to 180–190°C (350–375°F), or until a cube of bread browns in 30 seconds. Deep-fry the noodles, a handful at a time, for a few seconds until puffed up. Remove with a slotted spoon and drain on kitchen paper.

when all the noodles are fried, put them in a large bowl and drizzle the sweet red sauce over them, working it in carefully with your hands until the crispy white noodles turn a pinky-brown. Pour off all but 1 tablespoon of the oil from the pan. Arrange the noodles on a serving dish.

heat the oil and stir-fry the tofu pieces briefly over a moderately high heat, then arrange on top of the noodles. Sprinkle with the sliced spring onion shoots and serve immediately.

Serves 4
Preparation time: *10 minutes, plus soaking*
Cooking time: *35 minutes*

Chiang Mai Noodles

175 g (6 oz) dried egg noodles

1 tablespoon groundnut oil

2 garlic cloves, finely chopped

2 tablespoons Red Curry Paste (see page 12)

¼ teaspoon crushed dried chillies

250 ml (8 fl oz) coconut milk

500 ml (17 fl oz) Vegetable Stock (see page 15)

¼ teaspoon ground turmeric

1½ teaspoons curry powder

2 tablespoons vegetarian nam pla (fish sauce) or soy sauce

15 g (½ oz) palm sugar or light muscovado sugar

25 g (1 oz) celery stick, chopped

25 g (1 oz) shallot, finely sliced

25 g (1 oz) red pepper, cored, deseeded and chopped

25 g (1 oz) dried shiitake mushrooms, soaked for 15–20 minutes in warm water, drained and sliced, hard stalks cut away and added to a stockpot

1 tablespoon Crushed Roasted Nuts (see page 248)

To serve

2 tablespoons lime juice, or to taste

25 g (1 oz) each pickled cabbage and shallot

cook the noodles in a saucepan of boiling water for 5–6 minutes. Drain and rinse under cold running water to prevent further cooking.

heat the oil in a wok or large frying pan and stir-fry the garlic over a moderate heat for 1 minute, or until golden. Add the curry paste and chillies and mix thoroughly. Pour in the coconut milk, stirring constantly, then bring to the boil and cook until the liquid thickens a little.

add the stock, turmeric, curry powder, nam pla or soy sauce and sugar and return to the boil. Reduce the heat and add the celery, shallot, red pepper, mushrooms and nuts. Return to the boil, then remove from the heat.

transfer the noodles to a large serving bowl and pour over the sauce. Sprinkle with the lime juice to taste and serve with the pickled cabbage and shallot.

Serves 4
Preparation time: *30 minutes*
Cooking time: *15 minutes*

Egg Noodles with Oyster Mushrooms

Sometimes known as abalone, oyster mushrooms are fan shaped and pale grey. They have a smooth texture and are widely available in supermarkets.

200 g (7 oz) dried egg noodles

2 tablespoons groundnut oil

3 garlic cloves, chopped

1 teaspoon palm sugar or light muscovado sugar

1 tablespoon soy sauce

1 tablespoon vegetarian nam pla (fish sauce) or soy sauce

½ teaspoon salt, or to taste

50 g (2 oz) oyster mushrooms, torn into pieces

½ onion, chopped

125 g (4 oz) mangetout

4 large fresh orange chillies, cut into fine strips

pepper (optional)

cook the noodles in a saucepan of boiling water for 5–6 minutes. Drain and rinse under cold running water to prevent further cooking.

heat the oil in a wok or large frying pan and stir-fry the garlic briefly, then add the noodles, sugar, soy sauce, nam pla or soy sauce and salt. Stir-fry vigorously over a high heat for 1 minute.

add the vegetables and chillies and stir-fry for 2–3 minutes, then reduce the heat and taste and adjust the seasoning, if necessary. Turn on to a serving dish and serve immediately.

Serves 4
Preparation time: *5 minutes*
Cooking time: *10–12 minutes*

Noodles with Vegetables

Use groundnut oil with this dish rather than a strongly flavoured oil like olive oil, which will dominate it.

250 g (8 oz) dried egg noodles

about 2 tablespoons groundnut oil

50 g (2 oz) leeks, sliced

25 g (1 oz) oyster mushrooms, torn into pieces

1 celery stick with leaves, chopped

125 g (4 oz) Chinese leaves, sliced

25 g (1 oz) cauliflower florets

2 tablespoons soy sauce

1½ tablespoons palm sugar or light muscovado sugar

½ teaspoon salt, or to taste

1 teaspoon pepper, or to taste

2 tablespoons Crispy Garlic (see page 250)

fresh coriander leaves, to garnish

cook the noodles in a saucepan of boiling water for 5–6 minutes. Drain and rinse under cold running water to prevent further cooking.

heat the oil in a wok or large frying pan over a moderate heat, then add all of the ingredients, in turn, including the noodles, stir-frying briefly after each addition. Stir-fry for 3–4 minutes, adding more oil, if necessary. Taste and adjust the seasoning, if necessary.

transfer to a warm serving dish, garnish with coriander leaves and serve immediately.

Serves 4
Preparation time: *8 minutes*
Cooking time: *about 10 minutes*

Noodles with Fish Curry Topping

250 g (8 oz) cod fillets

250 ml (8 fl oz) water

1 litre (1¾ pints) coconut milk

3 tablespoons Red Curry Paste (see page 12)

3 tablespoons nam pla (fish sauce)

200 g (7 oz) dried thick noodles

125 g (4 oz) green beans

125 g (4 oz) fresh bean sprouts

125 ml (4 fl oz) coconut cream

To garnish

1 fresh red chilli, deseeded and finely sliced

25 g (1 oz) basil leaves

put the fish in a saucepan with the measurement water and bring to the boil. Reduce the heat and simmer for 8–10 minutes, or until the fish flakes easily when tested with a fork. Remove the fish from the saucepan with a slotted spoon, reserving the stock. Discard the skin and flake the flesh.

transfer the flaked fish to a clean saucepan with the coconut milk. Bring to just below boiling point and stir in the reserved fish stock.

add the curry paste to the fish mixture, together with the nam pla. Simmer for 15 minutes, stirring occasionally.

meanwhile, bring 2 large saucepans of water to the boil. Add the noodles to the first and cook for 10 minutes. For the last 3 minutes of cooking, add the green beans and bean sprouts to the second pan and boil for 2–3 minutes and 1 minute respectively. Drain all 3 ingredients thoroughly, rinse under cold running water and drain again.

with clean hands, carefully scoop the noodles into loose nest shapes, transfer to a large serving plate with the green beans and bean sprouts and warm through in a preheated oven, 160°C (325°F), Gas Mark 3.

when the fish curry has thickened and a thin film of oil appears on the surface, stir in the coconut cream. Bring to the boil, then remove from the heat and spoon over the noodles. Serve immediately, with the green beans and bean sprouts, garnished with sliced red chilli and basil leaves.

Serves 4
Preparation time: *20 minutes*
Cooking time: *25 minutes*

Rice Vermicelli in Coconut Milk

250 g (8 oz) dried rice vermicelli

2 teaspoons vegetable oil

2 eggs, beaten

500 ml (17 fl oz) coconut milk

½ onion, roughly chopped

250 g (8 oz) raw large prawns, peeled and deveined

4 tablespoons salted soya bean flavouring

2 tablespoons palm sugar or light muscovado sugar

1 tablespoon lemon juice

300 g (10 oz) fresh bean sprouts

125 g (4 oz) spring onions, chopped, plus very fine strips of spring onion to garnish

To garnish

3 tablespoons chopped fresh coriander leaves

2 fresh red chillies, deseeded and cut into fine strips

soak the vermicelli in a bowl of hot water for 15–20 minutes, then drain. Bring a large saucepan of water to the boil, add the vermicelli and cook, stirring occasionally, for 15 minutes. Drain well and set aside.

heat the oil in an omelette pan or small frying pan and add the eggs. Tilt the pan to form an omelette, lifting the sides of the omelette to allow any uncooked egg mixture to flow underneath. Remove the cooked, set omelette from the pan and slice it into thin shreds. Keep warm.

pour the coconut milk into a wok or saucepan and bring to the boil. Cook over a high heat for 10 minutes, or until a film of oil forms on the surface. Stir in the onion, prawns, soya bean flavouring, sugar and lemon juice. Cook for 5 minutes, then transfer half the mixture to a bowl and keep warm.

add the reserved vermicelli to the mixture in the pan. Mix well and cook for 5 minutes. Stir in half the bean sprouts and spring onions.

pile the vermicelli mixture on to a serving dish and top with the reserved prawn mixture and shredded omelette. Garnish with the chopped coriander, fine strips of red chilli and very fine strips of spring onion and serve with the remaining bean sprouts and spring onions.

Serves 4
Preparation time: *15 minutes, plus soaking*
Cooking time: *45 minutes*

Fried Rice with Seafood

Fried rice dishes always use rice that has been cooked and left over from a previous meal. This delicious mixture of seafood with fried rice is a typical seaside dish, available all along the coasts of Thailand.

3 tablespoons sunflower oil

4 garlic cloves, finely chopped

500 g (1 lb) mixed seafood, such as raw peeled prawns, shelled, cleaned scallops, cleaned squid and skinned white fish fillet

1 kg (2 lb) cold boiled rice

2 onions, sliced

2.5 cm (1 inch) fresh root ginger, peeled and finely sliced

2½ tablespoons soy sauce

3 spring onions, finely sliced

To garnish

1 long fresh red or green chilli, deseeded and finely sliced

fresh coriander leaves (optional)

heat the oil in a wok or large frying pan and stir-fry the garlic over a moderate heat for 1 minute, or until golden.

add the mixed seafood to the pan and stir-fry over a high heat for 1–2 minutes. Add the rice, onions, ginger and soy sauce and stir-fry for 3–4 minutes. Stir in the spring onions.

spoon the mixture on to a serving plate, garnish with the sliced chilli and a few coriander leaves, if liked, and serve immediately.

Serves 4
Preparation time: *10 minutes*
Cooking time: *5–7 minutes*

Egg-fried Noodles

This dish might almost be regarded as Thailand's standard noodle recipe. It is quick and easy to prepare and is usually offered as a secondary rather than a main dish.

4 tablespoons groundnut oil

1 garlic clove, crushed

1 shallot or small onion, thinly sliced

125 g (4 oz) fresh egg noodles

grated rind of 1 lime

2 teaspoons soy sauce

2 tablespoons lime juice

125 g (4 oz) boneless, skinless chicken breast or pork fillet, sliced

125 g (4 oz) raw crab meat or cleaned squid, cut into strips

125 g (4 oz) raw peeled prawns

1 tablespoon yellow soya bean paste

1 tablespoon nam pla (fish sauce)

2 tablespoons palm sugar or light muscovado sugar

2 eggs

2 fresh red chillies, deseeded and chopped

pepper

To garnish

fresh coriander leaves

finely pared lime rind

heat half the oil in a wok or large frying pan and stir-fry the garlic and shallot or onion over a moderate heat until soft and golden.

plunge the egg noodles into a saucepan of boiling water and leave to stand for a few seconds. Drain well and then add to the pan. Stir-fry with the grated lime rind, soy sauce and lime juice for 3–4 minutes. Remove, drain and keep warm.

heat the remaining oil in the pan and stir-fry the chicken or pork, crab meat or squid and prawns over a high heat until cooked through. Season with pepper and stir in the soya bean paste, nam pla and sugar.

break the eggs into the pan and stir gently until the mixture sets. Add the chillies and taste and adjust the seasoning, if necessary. Stir in the noodles and heat through over a low heat. Serve immediately, garnished with coriander leaves and finely pared lime rind.

Serves 4
Preparation time: *10 minutes*
Cooking time: *20 minutes*

Noodles with Chicken and Prawns

4 tablespoons vegetable oil

2 garlic cloves, crushed

125 g (4 oz) cooked fresh or dried egg noodles

2 tablespoons dark soy sauce

125 g (4 oz) mixed raw sliced boneless, skinless chicken breast and cleaned squid, and whole peeled prawns

½ teaspoon pepper

2 tablespoons nam pla (fish sauce)

125 g (4 oz) mixed shredded cabbage and broccoli florets

300 ml (½ pint) Chicken Stock (see page 14)

1 tablespoon cornflour

2 tablespoons water

2 tablespoons palm sugar or light muscovado sugar

heat half the oil in a wok or large frying pan and stir-fry half the garlic over a moderate heat for 1 minute, or until golden. Add the noodles and half the soy sauce and stir-fry for 3–5 minutes. Transfer to a serving dish and keep warm.

heat the remaining oil in the pan and stir-fry the remaining garlic over a moderate heat for 1 minute, or until golden. Add the chicken breast, squid, prawns, pepper and nam pla and stir-fry for 5 minutes.

add the shredded cabbage and broccoli florets to the pan and stir-fry for 3 minutes.

stir in the stock. Blend the cornflour with the measurement water and stir into the pan. Add the remaining soy sauce and sugar and bring to the boil. Reduce the heat and cook, stirring constantly, for 3 minutes. Pour the thickened sauce over the noodles and serve immediately.

Serves 4
Preparation time: *10 minutes*
Cooking time: *20 minutes*

Fried Noodles with Chicken and Broccoli

1½ tablespoons vegetable oil

1 large garlic clove, chopped

¼ onion, chopped

125 g (4 oz) boneless, skinless chicken breast, chopped

1 egg

150 g (5 oz) dried rice vermicelli, soaked in hot water for 15–20 minutes and drained

1½ tablespoons palm sugar or light muscovado sugar

1 tablespoon tamarind water (see page 32) or distilled white vinegar

5 tablespoons soy sauce

75 g (3 oz) broccoli florets and stalks

1 tablespoon chopped red pepper

75 g (3 oz) spring onions, chopped

50 g (2 oz) fresh bean sprouts

2 tablespoons Crushed Roasted Nuts (see page 248)

½ teaspoon pepper

fresh coriander leaves, to garnish

heat the oil in a wok or large frying pan and stir-fry the garlic, onion and chicken over a high heat for 2 minutes.

reduce the heat and break the egg into the mixture, stirring constantly. Add the vermicelli, sugar, tamarind water or vinegar, soy sauce and broccoli and stir-fry for 2 minutes.

add all the remaining ingredients, increase the heat and stir-fry vigorously for about 2 minutes.

turn the noodle mixture on to a serving dish, garnish with coriander leaves and serve immediately.

Serves 4
Preparation time: *10 minutes, plus soaking*
Cooking time: *6–7 minutes*

Vermicelli Noodles with Sauce

Although fresh root ginger is a good substitute if you cannot find galangal, never use dried ground ginger in Thai dishes.

500 g (1 lb) dried rice vermicelli

125 g (4 oz) ready-fried tofu, sliced, plus extra to garnish

1 tablespoon Red Curry Paste (see page 12)

50 g (2 oz) fresh galangal or root ginger, peeled and chopped

250 ml (8 fl oz) coconut milk

1½ teaspoons salt

300 ml (½ pint) hot water

2 teaspoons palm sugar or light muscovado sugar

To garnish

chopped fresh coriander leaves

1 fresh red chilli, finely sliced

soak the vermicelli in a bowl of hot water for 15–20 minutes.

meanwhile, put the tofu, curry paste, galangal or ginger, coconut milk and salt in a food processor and process until smooth. Add the measurement hot water and process again for 5 seconds.

pour the blended mixture into a saucepan and bring to the boil, stirring constantly. Reduce the heat to a simmer and add the sugar. Cook gently for a further 3–4 minutes.

drain the vermicelli and transfer to a warm serving bowl. Pour over the sauce and garnish with chopped coriander, tofu slices and sliced red chilli. Serve immediately.

Serves 4–6
Preparation time: *10 minutes, plus soaking*
Cooking time: *about 10 minutes*

Noodle Salad

For a hotter version of this popular dish, add five small bird's eye chillies to the sauce.

200 g (7 oz) dried thick noodles

Fish balls

300 g (10 oz) cod fillets, cooked, skinned and flaked

1 tablespoon Red Curry Paste (see page 12)

1 tablespoon chopped fresh coriander leaves, plus an extra sprig to garnish

1 teaspoon salt

1 tablespoon water

250 ml (8 fl oz) coconut milk

4 tablespoons nam pla (fish sauce)

4 heaped teaspoons palm sugar or light muscovado sugar

To garnish

1/3 red, 1/3 yellow and 1/3 green pepper, cored, deseeded and sliced into fine strips

1 tablespoon finely sliced fresh root ginger

To serve

5 cm (2 inch) piece of fresh root ginger, peeled and finely sliced

3 garlic cloves, finely sliced

2 tablespoons ground dried shrimp

bring a large saucepan of water to the boil, add the noodles and cook for 10 minutes. Drain thoroughly, rinse under cold running water and drain again. With clean hands, carefully scoop the noodles into loose nest shapes, transfer to a large serving plate and warm through in a preheated oven, 160°C (325°F), Gas Mark 3.

make the fish balls. Mix the cod, curry paste, chopped coriander, salt and measurement water together in a bowl. Form the mixture into 40 balls and set aside.

bring the coconut milk to the boil in a medium saucepan and add the fish balls, a few at a time, so that the milk continues to boil. Cook for about 4–5 minutes, turning over halfway through the cooking time. As each ball cooks, remove it with a slotted spoon and drain on a wire rack set over a tray. Leave to cool. Reserve the coconut milk.

arrange the cooked fish balls on top of the noodles and sprinkle with the ginger, garlic and ground dried shrimp. Combine the reserved coconut milk with the nam pla and sugar. Pour the spiced milk over the top of the fish balls and garnish with fine strips of red, yellow and green pepper, finely sliced ginger and a coriander sprig. Serve immediately.

Serves 4
Preparation time: *10 minutes*
Cooking time: *25 minutes*

Desserts

Fresh Fruit Platter

Desserts are not routinely offered after a Thai meal, but a fresh fruit salad is always welcome. Use whatever fruits are in season.

2 ripe mangoes

1 small ripe papaya

250 g (8 oz) fresh lychees

1 slice of watermelon

1 lime, cut into quarters

peel and thickly slice the mangoes, discarding the stones. Peel the papaya, scoop out the seeds and cut the flesh into 4 or 8 pieces.

peel the lychees and remove the stones. Peel the watermelon and cut the flesh into chunks, removing as many of the seeds as you can.

arrange the fruit on a serving plate, with the lime quarters ready to squeeze over the papaya.

Serves 4
Preparation time: *15–20 minutes*

Bananas in Coconut Milk

Thai cooks can choose between more than 20 varieties of banana, but in the West most food stores offer only two. If possible, use small, sweet fruits, rather than the larger, blander type.

200 ml (7 fl oz) coconut milk

100 ml (3½ fl oz) water

3 tablespoons palm sugar or light muscovado sugar

1 large or 2 small bananas, peeled, halved lengthways and each half cut into 4 pieces

put the coconut milk, measurement water and sugar in a saucepan and simmer, stirring occasionally, for about 6 minutes.

add the bananas and cook for 4 minutes, or until heated through. Serve the bananas hot or cold with the milk poured around them.

Serves 4
Preparation time: *2 minutes*
Cooking time: *10 minutes*

Coconut Balls

In Thailand, cooks often add food colouring to this mixture to jazz up the appearance a little. Yellow and pink are popular.

300 ml (½ pint) water

300 g (10 oz) palm sugar or light muscovado sugar

250 g (8 oz) grated fresh coconut or desiccated coconut, softened with a little cold water

mint sprigs, to decorate

put the measurement water and sugar in a saucepan and bring to the boil, stirring, until the sugar dissolves. Boil, without stirring, for 5 minutes, or until a thick sugar syrup forms. Add the coconut and continue boiling until the syrup has almost all evaporated.

put 12 tablespoonfuls of the mixture on a baking sheet, shaping each spoonful into a ball as you go.

leave to cool and harden for about 1½ hours. Serve in bowls, decorated with mint sprigs.

Makes 12
Preparation time: *15 minutes, plus cooling and setting*
Cooking time: *20 minutes*

Mango and Sticky Rice

Sticky rice, sometimes called glutinous rice, is a type of short-grain rice used in many Thai desserts. It must be soaked before use and then steamed, never boiled.

500 g (1 lb) sticky (glutinous) rice

150 g (5 oz) palm sugar or light muscovado sugar

300 ml (½ pint) coconut milk

2 ripe mangoes

soak the rice for at least 6 hours or overnight. Drain and rinse the rice well, then cook in a steamer for about 30 minutes. Give the rice a good shake halfway through steaming to make sure that it is evenly cooked.

meanwhile, combine the sugar and coconut milk in a large bowl and stir well.

when the rice is cooked, transfer it to the coconut mixture and stir thoroughly for 2–3 minutes to achieve a creamy consistency. Cover with a lid and leave to stand at room temperature for 30 minutes.

peel and slice the mangoes, discarding the stones, and serve arranged attractively on a dish with the rice.

Serves 4
Preparation time: *10 minutes, plus soaking and standing*
Cooking time: *30 minutes*

Banana Fritters

You could serve the fritters with ice cream, but a more traditional accompaniment would be a caramel sauce made with palm sugar, water and a little coconut milk.

about 750 ml (1¼ pints) groundnut oil, for deep-frying

750 g (1½ lb) bananas

caster sugar, to serve

Batter

200 ml (7 fl oz) water

150 g (5 oz) rice flour or plain flour

125 g (4 oz) grated fresh coconut or desiccated coconut

½ teaspoon salt

75 g (3 oz) palm sugar or light muscovado sugar

1 egg

make the batter. Beat all the batter ingredients together in a bowl.

heat the oil in a wok or deep frying pan to 180–190°C (350–375°F), or until a cube of bread browns in 30 seconds. Meanwhile, peel the bananas, cut each one lengthways into thirds, then cut each third crossways to make slices about 7 cm (3 inches) long.

coat the banana slices with the batter and slide them carefully into the hot oil, 3 or 4 at a time. Deep-fry for 3–4 minutes until golden brown. Remove with a slotted spoon and drain on kitchen paper.

when all the banana slices are cooked, arrange them on a serving dish and sprinkle with caster sugar. Serve immediately.

Serves 4
Preparation time: *8 minutes*
Cooking time: *about 10 minutes*

Coconut Cream Custard

Using bowls made from banana leaves would be a spectacular way of serving this dessert, but if you are afraid that the bowls might leak, use ramekins wrapped in banana leaves and tied with string.

2 large eggs

200 ml (7 fl oz) coconut milk

175 g (6 oz) palm sugar or light muscovado sugar

¼ teaspoon salt

2 banana leaves, formed into 4 bowls (optional)

desiccated coconut or grated fresh coconut, to decorate

beat the eggs in a bowl. Add the coconut milk and sugar and beat well, then add the salt and beat again.

pour the mixture into 4 ramekins or, if you prefer, into banana leaf bowls. Transfer the filled ramekins or banana leaf bowls to a steamer and steam for 15–20 minutes.

serve warm, decorated with desiccated or grated coconut.

Serves 4
Preparation time: *5 minutes*
Cooking time: *15–20 minutes*

Mung Bean Balls in Syrup

175 g (6 oz) shelled split mung beans

2 litres (3½ pints) water

250 ml (8 fl oz) coconut milk

925 g (1 lb 14 oz) palm sugar or light muscovado sugar

1 teaspoon vanilla extract

20 egg yolks, lightly beaten

To decorate

icing sugar

nasturtiums, pansies or other edible flower petals

wash the beans under cold running water until the water runs clear. Transfer the beans to a large saucepan, add 1.5 litres (2½ pints) of the measurement water and bring to the boil. Reduce the heat and simmer for 20 minutes.

drain the beans thoroughly and return them to a clean saucepan with the coconut milk and 175 g (6 oz) of the sugar.

cook the mixture over a low heat, stirring constantly, until it is thick and dry enough to be shaped. To test if the mixture is the right consistency, remove it from the heat, leave to cool slightly, then prod gently with a clean finger. If the mixture does not stick to your finger, it is ready. Beat in the vanilla extract and leave to cool.

when the mixture is cold, form it into ovals, about 1–2.5 cm (½–1 inch) long, and set aside.

put the remaining measurement water in a large saucepan with the remaining sugar and bring to the boil, stirring, until all the sugar dissolves. Boil, without stirring, for 5 minutes.

remove the sugar syrup from the heat. Dip the mung bean balls in the beaten egg yolks, then add them to the syrup. When the surface of the syrup is covered with coated balls, return the pan to the heat and bring the syrup to the boil. Boil for 5 minutes, turning the balls over halfway through cooking. When the balls are cooked, transfer to a serving dish with a slotted spoon. Repeat until all the balls are cooked. Serve hot or cold, sprinkled with icing sugar and scattered with edible flower petals.

Serves 4
Preparation time: *15 minutes, plus cooling*
Cooking time: *45 minutes*

Golden Threads in Syrup

1 egg

11 egg yolks

500 ml (17 fl oz) water

750 g (1½ lb) palm sugar or light muscovado sugar

To serve

diced dried papaya

mint sprigs

finely grated fresh coconut (optional)

mix the egg and egg yolks together in a large bowl. Beat with a hand-held electric mixer or a wire whisk until frothy, then strain into a large jug.

combine the measurement water and sugar in a saucepan and bring to the boil, stirring until the sugar dissolves. Boil, without stirring, for 5 minutes.

make the threads. Fill a plastic piping bag fitted with a fine writing nozzle with the egg mixture, or use a greaseproof paper cone with the very tip snipped off, and block the nozzle or hole with your fingertip. Hold it over the boiling syrup, remove your finger and drizzle the egg mixture into the syrup using a spiral movement in one direction only. Try not to break the thread. As soon as the threads are cooked (they cook very quickly), remove with a slotted spoon and drain on kitchen paper.

repeat with the remaining egg mixture, adding a little water if the syrup becomes too thick.

serve immediately with the diced dried papaya and mint sprigs, topped with grated coconut, if liked.

Serves 4
Preparation time: *5 minutes*
Cooking time: *10 minutes*

Fried Apple and Coconut Cakes

You can prevent the apple rings from turning brown while you work by dropping them into a bowl of acidulated water. Pat them dry on kitchen paper before adding them to the batter.

100 g (3½ oz) palm sugar or light muscovado sugar

450 ml (¾ pint) water

300 g (10 oz) rice flour

1 egg

2 teaspoons baking powder

pinch of salt

125 g (4 oz) grated fresh coconut or desiccated coconut

4 apples

oil, for deep-frying

icing sugar, to decorate

crème fraîche, to serve

put the sugar and measurement water in a saucepan and heat over a low heat, stirring constantly, until the sugar dissolves. Bring to the boil, then stir gently for 2–3 minutes until syrupy. Remove from the heat and leave to cool.

mix together the flour, egg, baking powder, salt and coconut in a large bowl to form a smooth paste.

pour the cooled syrup into the flour paste mixture and beat to form a smooth batter. Cover and leave to stand for 20 minutes.

core the apples and cut them into rings. Add to the batter.

heat the oil in a wok or deep frying pan to 180–190°C (350–375°F), or until a cube of bread browns in 30 seconds. Deep-fry the apple rings, in batches, until golden brown on both sides, turning once. Remove with a slotted spoon and drain on kitchen paper.

dust the apple rings with icing sugar and serve hot with crème fraîche.

Serves 4
Preparation time: *20 minutes, plus cooling and standing*
Cooking time: *about 15 minutes*

Silom Sunrise

If you are planning a special dinner party, make it go with an extra swing by offering your guests this delicious drink.

2 ripe mangoes, peeled, stoned and sliced

125 ml (4 fl oz) tequila

50 ml (2 fl oz) Triple Sec

25 ml (1 fl oz) grenadine

75 ml (3 fl oz) lime or lemon juice

75 ml (3 fl oz) sugar syrup

6 ice cubes, crushed

lime or lemon slices, to serve

put all the ingredients in a blender and blend until the ice is crushed.

serve in pretty glasses, decorated with lime or lemon slices.

Serves 4
Preparation time: *10–12 minutes*

clipboard: Although you can get canned and dried mangoes, use fresh, ripe fruits for this recipe. Cut the mangoes lengthways either side of the large, flat stone before you slice the flesh.

Sauces and Garnishes

Lime and Fish Sauce

6 tablespoons lime juice

2 teaspoons palm sugar or light muscovado sugar

½–1 teaspoon nam pla (fish sauce)

½ teaspoon finely chopped shallot

1 teaspoon finely chopped fresh red chilli

squeeze the lime juice into a small bowl and add the sugar. Mix well until the sugar dissolves.

add the remaining ingredients and serve as a dipping sauce.

Preparation time: *4–5 minutes*

Hot Sweet Sauce

100 ml (3½ fl oz) distilled white vinegar or Chinese rice vinegar

65 g (2½ oz) palm sugar or light muscovado sugar

¼ teaspoon salt

1 small fresh green chilli, finely chopped

1 small fresh red chilli, finely chopped

pour the vinegar into a small saucepan and heat over a low heat. Add the sugar and salt and cook, stirring, until the sugar dissolves. Remove from the heat and leave to cool.

pour the sauce into a small bowl and stir in the chopped chillies.

Preparation time: *2 minutes*
Cooking time: *1–2 minutes*

Crispy Basil and Crispy Mint

2 tablespoons groundnut oil

25 g (1 oz) basil or mint leaves

1 small fresh red chilli, finely sliced

heat the oil in a wok or large frying pan and stir-fry the herb leaves and chilli over a moderately high heat for 1 minute until crispy. Remove with a slotted spoon and drain on kitchen paper.

Preparation time: *2 minutes*
Cooking time: *1 minute*

Crushed Roasted Nuts

25 g (1 oz) unroasted, unsalted peanuts or cashew nuts

dry-fry the nuts in a frying pan, using no oil, stirring constantly, until golden brown. Remove from the heat and leave to cool.

put the nuts in a plastic bag and use a rolling pin to break them into small pieces.

Preparation time: *2 minutes*
Cooking time: *3–5 minutes*

Ground Roast Rice

25 g (1 oz) uncooked rice

dry-fry the rice in a frying pan, using no oil, shaking and stirring constantly, until golden-brown. Remove from the heat and leave to cool.

grind the rice in a clean coffee or spice grinder or in a mortar with a pestle.

Preparation time: *2 minutes*
Cooking time: *3–5 minutes*

Garlic Oil

4 tablespoons vegetable or sunflower oil

I tablespoon crushed garlic

heat the oil in a small frying pan and add the crushed garlic.

cook over a low heat, stirring occasionally, until the garlic is golden. Use in recipes as required.

Garlic Mixture

2 tablespoons crushed garlic

2 tablespoons chopped fresh coriander root or stalk

½ tablespoon pepper

put all the ingredients in a mortar and pound with a pestle to a paste.

Crispy Garlic and Crispy Shallots

about 750 ml (1¼ pints) groundnut oil, for deep-frying

25 g (1 oz) garlic, finely chopped

25 g (1 oz) shallots, finely chopped

heat the oil in a wok or large frying pan and stir-fry the garlic over a moderately high heat for about 40 seconds until golden.

remove the garlic with a slotted spoon, draining as much oil as possible back into the wok, then spread out on kitchen paper to drain. Repeat with the shallots, stir-frying for 1½–2 minutes.

when the garlic and shallots are dried and crispy, you can store them in separate airtight containers, where they will keep for up to 1 month. When the oil is cold, return it to an airtight container, to be reused.

Preparation time: *5 minutes*
Cooking time: *2–3 minutes*

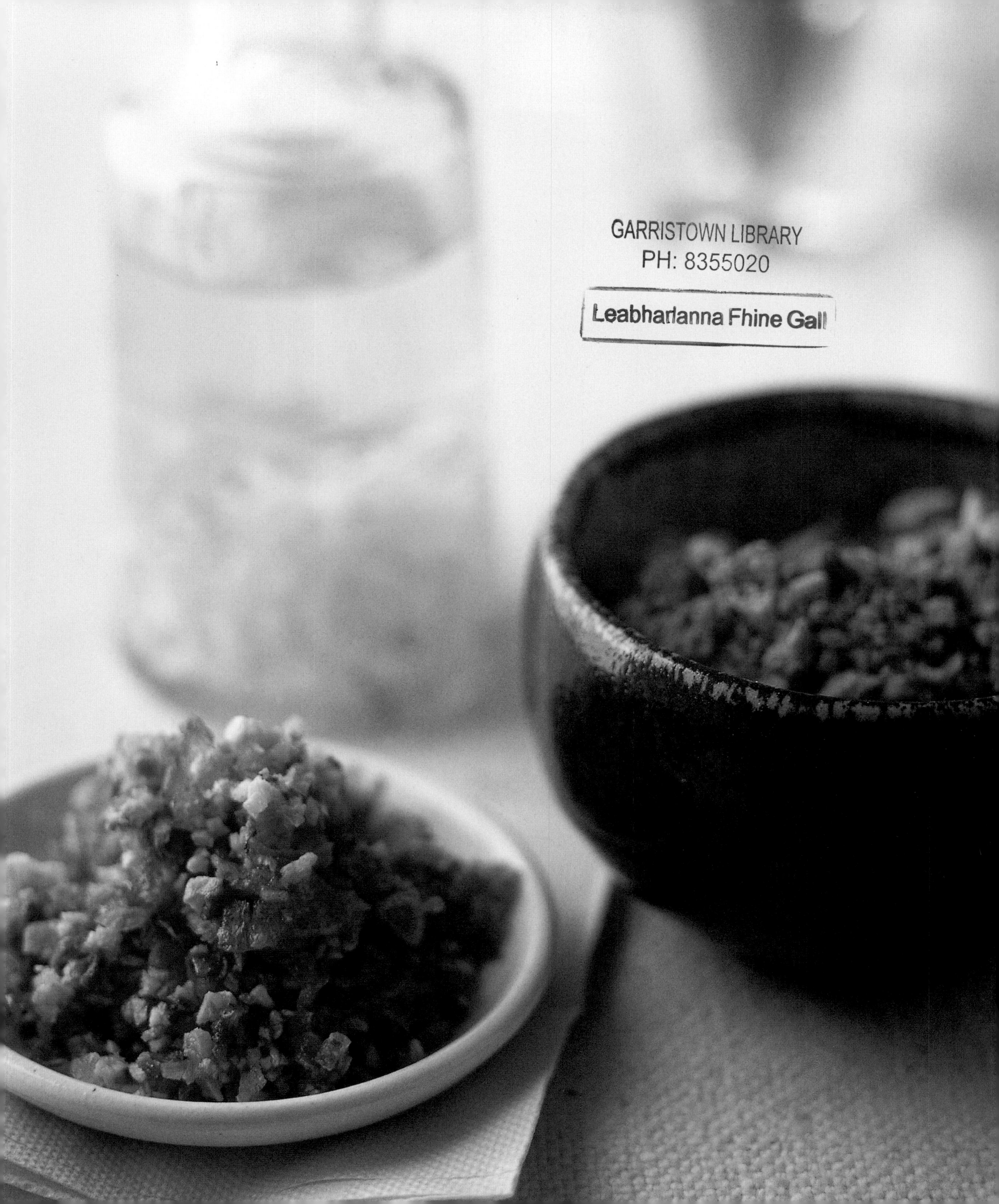

Index

Acknowledgements

Main photography ©Octopus Publishing Group Limited/Sandra Lane.

Other photography:
Octopus Publishing Group Limited/David Loftus 97, 153, 183; /Neil Mersh 41, 43, 101, 125, 155, 169, 179, 181, 215, 241; /Peter Myers 47, 49, 73, 91, 93, 135, 137, 139, 143, 161, 163, 167, 173, 177, 207, 221, 239; /William Reavell 12, 16, 18, 53, 149 bottom right, 149 top left, 211; /Philip Webb 51.

Executive Editor **Nicky Hill**
Editor **Jessica Cowie**
Executive Art Editor **Darren Southern**
Designer **'ome design**
Picture Researcher **Sophie Delpech**
Senior Production Controller **Martin Croshaw**